# PRINCIPIA THEOLOGIÆ FANATICÆ (1619)
## (*PRINCIPLES OF THE FANATIC THEOLOGY*)

WHICH THEOPHRASTUS PARACELSUS FATHERED,
WHICH WEIGEL POLISHED;

AS THESE WERE REDUCED UNDER EXAMINATION TO
BRIEF THESES
and
PRESENTED FOR SOLEMN DEBATE
WITH THE HELP OF GOD, THRICE *OPTIMUS MAXIMUS*,

by
**NICOLAUS HUNNIUS**,
DOCTOR OF THEOLOGY AND PUBLIC PROFESSOR

As translated by Rev. Dr. Richard J. Dinda, Prof. Em.

Introduction and notes by Rt. Rev. James D. Heiser, M.Div., S.T.M.

Repristination Press
Malone, Texas

Translation © 2005 by Richard Dinda. Published by permission of the translator. No part of this publication may be reproduced, stored in a retrieval system, or transmitted in any form or by any means, electronic, mechanical, photocopying or otherwise without the prior written permission of Repristination Press.

Published in 2015.

REPRISTINATION PRESS
P.O. BOX 173
BYNUM, TEXAS 76631

www.repristinationpress.com

ISBN 1-891469-27-4

# The Historical Context of N. Hunnius' Principia Theologiæ Fanaticæ (1619)

## Introduction

Even among Confessional Lutherans, a detailed knowledge of the Age of Lutheran Orthodoxy (1580–1713)—its most significant teachers, and their primary contributions to theological literature—is something which cannot be taken for granted. The period has been largely neglected in the course of seminary education in most Lutheran seminaries in the English-speaking world and thus it is hardly surprising when non-Lutherans pay it similar courtesy. As interest in, and study of, the Book of Concord (1580) has declined throughout the broad constellation of church bodies which have inherited the name—if not the substance—of the Evangelical Lutheran Church, so it is little wonder that the era most clearly defined by the *Concordia* is largely neglected.

Still, efforts by several publishing houses over the past few decades have raised a certain degree of awareness regarding several of the first tier of theologians of that era by publishing several of the more important theological tomes from the Age of Lutheran Orthodoxy, so that dogmatic and devotional works by Johann Gerhard (1582–1637)[1], as well as a few writings by J.A.A. Quenstedt (1617–1688)[2] and even—

---

[1] Examples range from his *Comprehensive Explanation of Holy Baptism and the Lord's Supper (1610)* (Malone, Texas: Repristination Press, 2000) and his *Daily Exercise of Piety* (Malone, Texas: Repristination Press, 1994) to his *Loci Theologici* (St. Louis: Concordia Publishing House, 2005–).

[2] Thus far, several chapters from Quenstedt's have been published, including: *The Nature and Character of Theology: An Introduction to the Thought of J.A. Quenstedt* (St. Louis: Concordia Publishing House, 1986) and *The Church (Theologica Didactico-Polemica, Part IV, Chapter XV: De ecclesia)* (Malone, Texas: Repristination Press, 1999).

perhaps somewhat quixotically—some of the writings of Valerius Herberger (1562-1627)[3] have been translated into English.

Nicolaus Hunnius (1585-1643) ranks among the more significant theologians of the Age of Lutheran Orthodoxy, but his writings have been largely overlooked in this translation effort—a development which is intriguing, since earlier generations of American Lutherans placed great value on his work.[4] To date, however, only one of Hunnius' works—his *Diaskepsis Theologica* (1626)—has been published previously in a modern edition.[5] Therefore, given the general lack of familiarity with Hunnius' life and work, a few words of introduction are in order.

Nicolaus Hunnius was the third son of Aegidius Hunnius (1550-1603), another notable Lutheran theologian, who was the superintendent of Saxony and a professor at the University of Wittenberg. An instructor in philosophy and theology by the age of 24, Nicolaus Hunnius went on to receive his doctorate in 1612 and was called by the elector of Saxony to serve as superintendent of Eilenburg. Hunnius returned to academia in 1617 when the elector of Saxony called him to the University of Wittenberg to fill the vacancy left by the death of Leonard Hütter (1563-1616). However, Hunnius did not remain in academia for long; in 1623, he accepted the call to serve as superintendent of Lübeck. Hunnius has the distinction of being the only major theologian of the Age of Lu-

---

3 e.g., *Great Works of God: Genesis Parts 1 and 2*, trans. by Matthew Carver (St. Louis: Concordia Publishing House, 2010).

4 C.F.W. Walther recommended three works from the Age of Orthodoxy in his Lutheran theological library for pastors: Johann Gerhard's *Loci Theologici*, J.W. Baier's *Compendium*, and Nicolaus Hunnius' *Glaubenslehre*, that is, his *Epitome credendorum*. (*Lehre und Wehre*, vol. 1, p. 264 and 341 as cited by F. A. Schmidt in "Intuitu Fidei," *The Error in Modern Missouri: Its Inception, Development, and Refutation*, trans. R.C.H. Lenski, (Columbus: Lutheran Book Concern, 1897) ed. by George H. Schodde, p. 441.

5 *Diaskepsis Theologica: A theological examination of the fundamental difference between Evangelical Lutheran doctrine and Calvinist or Reformed teaching* (Malone, Texas: Repristination Press, 2001).

theran Orthodoxy to leave the university not only once, but twice, to serve an altar and pulpit in the ministry of Word and Sacrament.

The most fruitful years of Nicolaus Hunnius' ministry appear to be those which he spent as superintendent (bishop) of the Hanseatic city of Lübeck. Indeed, it was after his call to Lübeck in 1623 that the bulk of Hunnius' written work was published, including his *Epitome credendorum* (1625), *Apostasia ecclesiæ Romanæ* (1632) and the aforementioned *Diaskepsis theologica* (1626). However, Hunnius' endeavors in Lübeck were hardly limited to writing. Hunnius "revitalized the somewhat moribund *Ministerium tripolitanum* of Luebeck, Hamburg and Lueneburg in order to mount a combined offensive against the three enemies of Lutheranism in these North German mercantile communities: the ... enthusiasts; the increasingly large Reformed communities; and the Roman Catholic missionaries."[6] Additionally, Hunnius carried out numerous other reforms of the Church in Lübeck which refute the myth of 'dead' orthodoxy:

> He reinstituted individual announcement for Holy Communion and regular catechetical examinations; defended the *regimen ecclesiasticum* of his clergy against the council's encroachments; proposed that the city engage a director of religious education; boldly attacked the vices of his Luebeck parishioners; promoted education; and founded an organization for the relief of clergymen's widows and orphans.[7]

### Hunnius' "Fanatics": Paracelsus and Weigel

The work under consideration at present—Hunnius' *Principia Theologiæ Fanaticæ (1619)*—belongs to the second period of its author's service at the University of Wittenberg, and its brevity belies its significance. Although little more

---

6 Arthur Carl Piepkorn, "Hunnius, Father and Son," in *The Encyclopedia of the Lutheran Church,* ed. by Julius Bodensieck, (Minneapolis: Augsburg Publishing House, 1965), 3 vols., vol. 2, p. 1065–1066.
7 ibid., p. 1066.

than a tract,[8] Hunnius' work constitutes the first formal response by one of the Lutheran fathers to the growing threat of late-Reformation/post-Reformation Spiritualism. Specifically, the "theological fanatics" which are the focus of Hunnius' examination are the followers of Theophrastus Bombastus von Hohenheim ( 1493-1541)—remembered today by his chosen sobriquet, "Paracelsus"—and Valentin Weigel (1533-1588). Paracelsus is remembered not only for his contributions to the field of medicine, but above all for his mystical theology—and it was, of course, this latter Paracelsian influence which was of interest to Nicolaus Hunnius.

The name of Valentin Weigel is undoubtedly less familiar today than that of Paracelsus, but his influence was profoundly significant in the realm of mystical theology[9]—an influence made all the more galling to a theologian of Hunnius' caliber, in that Weigel was a Lutheran pastor who had publicly subscribed to the *Book of Concord* (1580), at the same time that he generated a vast, private literature which directly attacked the theology confessed in the *Concordia*. Regarding the hypocrisy of his position, Weigel sets forth what is presumed to be an autobiographical passage in an 1584 work entitled *Dialogus de Christianismo:*

> I did not subscribe to their teaching or human books, but rather since their intention was aimed at the apostolic Scripture and the same is to be preferred to all human books, as it should be, I could suffer it. But had they placed one single other book above the Scriptures of the prophets and apostles, I would not have

---

8 The work is only 60 pages long, which would not be an unusual length for an introductory chapter in the books of that period.

9 "Weigel's existence has suffered eclipse in the tradition in which his work is a pivotal landmark. In the history of German mysticism, he stands halfway between Paracelsus (1493-1541) and Sabastian Franck (1499-1542) who were his dissenting forerunners and Jacob Boehme (1575-1624) who was the most important dissenter to follow after and resemble him." (Andrew Weeks, *Valentin Weigel—German Religious Dissenter, Speculative Theorist, and Advocate of Tolerance,* [Albany: State University of New York Press, 2000] p. 5)

agreed to it. Besides, it all [happened in] a rush or an overhastening, so that one wasn't permitted to think it over for several days or weeks. Instead, in a single hour they read off the entire convolute and demanded a signature right away. Third, I poor Auditor didn't see fit to prepare and serve a feast for the devil, [knowing] that the whole lot would have cried out: "There, there, we knew it all along: he is not in conformity with our doctrine!"[10]

Weigel's example is proof that the phenomenon of pastors taking a *quatenus* subscription to the *Book of Concord* is nothing new. Whatever the reservations Weigel maintained within his conscience, he served as the pastor of the Lutheran congregation in Zschopau, Saxony from 1567 until his death in 1588.[11]

### The Principia *in the Context of the Thirty Years War*

While considering Hunnius' *Principia*, it is important to remember the broader context of both the work and its author. In a very real sense, one may briefly summarize the historical context of the *Principia Theologiæ Fanaticæ* of Nicolaus Hunnius as the end of Christendom, in the sense that it appeared in print just as the death knell was sounding for an era which began with Constantine's Edict of Milan (A.D. 313). Such an evaluation would, in fact, be accepted even within the sphere of secular historical study, for the *Principia* was published at the beginning of that momentous—though, even now, poorly understood—period succinctly called the Thirty Years War (1618–1648). If 'Christendom' was still an operative concept at the beginning of that war, the same could not be said by its end.

Since the Peace of Augsburg in 1555, a truce had existed which permitted the appearance of Christendom to re-

---
10 Weeks, *Valentin Weigel—German Religious Dissenter*, p. 15.
11 ibid., p. 11.

main, albeit as a hollow shell. As Wilson observed in his recent history of the Thirty Years War:

> ... [T]he peace-makers of 1555 deliberately blurred the religious distinctions to maintain an element of the old universal ideal of a single Christendom. Lutherans were referred to as 'adherents of the Confession of Augsburg', without defining what that meant, while use of words like 'peace', 'religious belief' and 'reformation' were a deliberate attempt to incorporate values that all still shared, yet understood differently. For Lutherans, 'reformation' meant the right of legally constituted authorities to change religious practice in line with their founder's teachings. To Catholics, it confirmed their church's role in spiritual guidance.
>
> These ambiguities were carried over into the confessional element of the settlement. While France, Spain and the Dutch were still fighting to achieve victory for a single confession in their domains, the Empire agreed to recognize both Catholicism and Lutheranism at its territorial level. Contrary to the later impression, this did not leave the princes entirely free to choose between the two faiths. The formula 'he who rules, decides the religion' (*cuius regio, eius religio*) was not included in the text and emerged in debates about the treaty only after 1586. Rather than allowing perpetual change, the intention was to fix matters as they were mid-century.[12]

The Peace of Augsburg allowed the memory of Christendom to continue for a few generations, and it was not in vain. The Church of the Augsburg Confession had time to resolve its own controversies and make its own common confession in 1580 against those errors which had erupted since the death

---

12  Peter H. Wilson, *The Thirty Years War—Europe's Tragedy*, (Cambridge, Massachusetts: Harvard University Press, 2009) p. 41–42.

of Martin Luther. The Roman Church also reached its own common confession, as that was imposed in the final sessions of the Council of Trent, which came to its conclusion in 1563. However, the presence of the two irreconcilable confessions within one empire required that either the unity of the empire or the integrity of the respective confessions would be sacrificed.

Again, as Wilson observes, the treaties at the end of the war did not programmatically terminate Christendom, but it did recognize the divisions as permanent, and began opening the door to further secularization of European society:

> Rulers retained the 'right of Reformation' granted in 1555, but only as supervision of their territorial churches. They were no longer able to impose their own theological beliefs on their subjects. Any subsequent conversion was to remain a private matter. Rulers gained personal freedom of conscience but lost a key aspect of their political authority. ...
>
> Only the Habsburgs retained the full right of Reformation in its previous form, because the IPO [*Instrumentum Pacis Osnabrugense*] merely obliged them to respect the Protestant faith of the Lower Austrian nobility, the city of Breslau, and the Silesian princes and their tenants. Elsewhere, they remained free to suppress Protestant minorities, even if these had existed in 1624. ... Whereas half of Europe had been under Protestant rule in 1590, that proportion fell to a fifth a century later under the most significant Catholic gains made in the Habsburg monarchy.[13]

The aftermath of the Thirty Years War was thus a time of growing confessional chaos. The Peace of Westphalia declared in 1648 not only legalized Calvinism,[14] it released the restraints which had previously suppressed an occult under-

---
13 Wilson, p. 759.
14 ibid., p. 758.

current which had haunted the Reformation and post-Reformation eras. The understanding of the relationship between Church and State which emerged from the ashes of thirty years of butchery unveiled a state with an attenuated interest in upholding the confession of the faith, even as the secular authorities saw their own authority in more 'divine' terms as the power of the Church waned. Louis XIV (1638–1715)—the "Sun King"—typified the absolutist pretensions of secular authority deified in the pages of Thomas Hobbes' book, *The Leviathan (1651)*. In this new world, the forces of orthodoxy found themselves suddenly bereft of the powers of the State to suppress Spiritualism and Occultism—and it was not long before they were running rampant.

Hunnius' work gains added significance when one considers that, at the very moment when the armed might at the disposal of the Roman Church was threatening to sweep northward, he warned of a threat which was ultimately more dangerous than that posed by an invading army.

## Hermeticism and Cabalism, and Renaissance Spiritualism

No more than a cursory recounting of the influence Hermeticism and Cabalism in the Reformation era is possible in the current context. However, as has been documented elsewhere,[15] the study of the purported writings of Hermes Trismegistus and the Cabalistic study of the Sacred Scriptures may be counted among the more poisonous fruit of the Renaissance.

The writings attributed to the mythical figure of Hermes Trismegistus have been a troublesome form of Gnosticism which the Church has confronted since the days of the early church fathers.[16] Various legends grew up around Hermes

---
15 Heiser, *Prisci Theologi and the Hermetic Reformation in the Fifteenth Century* (Malone, Texas: Repristination Press, 2011).
16 See, for example, Florian Ebeling, *The Secret History of Hermes Trismegistus—Hermeticism from Ancient to Modern Times* trans. by David Lorton (Ithaca and London: Cornell University Press, 2007) p. 38–44.

Trismegistus—the more tame of which portrayed him as an Egyptian who was a contemporary of Moses.[17] However, other traditions provided him with an even more grand identification:

> In Hellenistic Egypt Hermes Trismegistus arose from a merging of the figures of Thoth and Hermes. ... In the fifth century Herodotus wrote that Hermes and Thoth corresponded to each other, for both were considered to be tricksters, and sometimes even thieves, who equipped with magical capabilities, were messengers of the gods and conductors of the dead. ...
> Was there only a single Hermes Trismegistus? A text attributed to Manetho, an Egyptians priest of the third century B.C.E., tells of two figures who bore the name Hermes. The Egyptian Thoth was the first Hermes; prior to the Flood he recorded his knowledge in hieroglyphs. After the Flood the knowledge was translated from the "sacred language" into Greek and placed in the temples by the second Hermes, the son of "Agathodaimon" and father of Tat. Cicero took multiplicity to the limit, reporting in his *On the Nature of the Gods* that there were five gods called Hermes, the last of whom was Hermes Trismegistus.
> God, prophet, or sage? In any event, writings bearing the name of Hermes Trismegistus were handed down, and these works established the Hermetic tradition.[18]

While some fathers such as Clement of Alexandria and Lactantius were somewhat favorable in their assessment of Hermes' writings, St. Augustine of Hippo recognized that Hermetic prophesies (and Hermetic magic) were irreconcilable with the Christian verity, and following the time of Augustine, the one known work attributed to Hermes—the *Asclepius*—was little threat to Christian orthodoxy.

---

17 For a comprehensive study of the changing 'face' of Hermes, see Antoine Faivre, *The Eternal Hermes—From Greek God to Alchemical Magus* (Grand Rapids: Phanes Press, 1995).
18 Ebeling, p. 6–7.

Hermes Trismegistus took on a new life in the days of the fifteenth century Italian Renaissance. Gemistos Pletho (1355-1454)[19]—a neopagan who served as a member of the Greek delegation to the Council of Ferrara-Florence—was in Florence in 1438 and 1439, and inspired Cosimo de'Medici with the idea of founding a Platonic Academy. The task of establishing the academy fell to the man chosen by Cosimo de'Medici: a young scholar by the name of Marsilio Ficino. Cosimo personally procured a collection of manuscripts now known as the *Corpus Hermeticum*, which he made Ficino's top priority for translation. In time, Ficino also translated works which were purportedly written by Orpheus and Zoroaster. Ficino also attempted a harmonization of Christian and Neoplatonic doctrine, a work which he entitled, *Theologia Platonica*.

Ficino believed that Zoroaster and Hermes Trismegistus were the first teachers in a succession of *Prisci Theologi*, "ancient theologians" who were divinely inspired, and who led the Gentiles in the way of salvation. In the promotion of the notion of such *Prisci Theologi*, Ficino was joined by Giovanni Pico della Mirandola (1463-1494), whose *Oration on the Dignity of Man* and *900 Theses* were written in defense of the divine inspiration of such ancient pagan teachers and promoted the study of a form of medieval Jewish gnosticized mysticism known as Cabala as a key to understanding the true meaning of Scripture.[20]

A third factor played into the framework which prepared for the Paracelsian and Weigelian mysticism: the millennial expectations of Joachim of Fiore (1135-1202). As Voegelin observes in *Science, Politics & Gnosticism*, "Joachim's historical speculation was directed against the then reigning philosophy of history of St. Augustine."[21] Unlike the earlier Christian belief that the

---

19 For Pletho's neopagan views, see C.M. Woodhouse, *Gemistos Plethon— The Last of the Hellenes* (Oxford: Clarendon Press, 2000).
20 For an extended examination of Pico's theology, see Heiser, *Prisci Theologi*, chapters two and four.
21 Eric Voegelin, *Science, Politics & Gnosticism*, (Wilmington, Delaware: ISI Books, 2004) p. 69.

world was nearing its end, awaiting the return of the Christ in glory, Joachim believed that a new, glorious age would soon arise:

> The first age lasted from the Creation to the birth of Christ; the second, that of the Son, began with Christ. But the age of the Son was not, as Augustine had it, mankind's last; rather, it was to be followed by an additional one, that of the Holy Spirit. We can recognize, even in this thoroughly Christian context, the first symptoms of the idea of a post-Christian era. Joachim went further and indulged in concrete speculations about the beginning of the age of the Holy Spirit, fixing its inauguration at 1260. And the new age, like the preceding ones, was to be ushered in by the appearance of a leader. As the first age began with Abraham and the second with Christ, so the third was to begin in the year 1260 with the appearance of a *dux e Babylone*.[22]

The fact that Joachim's third age failed to materialize in 1260 did not strip the notion of its mythological power. In his book, *The Pursuit of the Millennium*[23], Norman Cohn declares that Joachim's "new prophetic system" was "to be the most influential one known to Europe until the appearance of Marxism"[24]—and given that Karl Marx, in turn, also looked to an immanentized eschatology which was clearly influenced by Joachimite thought, it is possible to simply interpret Marxism's vision for the final condition of mankind as simply one more version of the "third age."[25] In Cohn's assessment:

22 Voegelin, p. 69–70.
23 (New York: Oxford University Press, 1970).
24 p. 108.
25 Igor Shafarevich maintains that early modern 'utopian Socialists'—including Thomas More and Tommaso Campanella—"borrows the idea derived from medieval mysticism (Joachim of Flore's for instance) that history is an immanent and orderly evolutionary process. However, the goal and the driving force invested in this process by the mystics—knowledge of God and merging with Him—is eliminated. Instead, *progress* is recognized as the motivating force of history, and human reason is

For the long-term, indirect influence of Joachim's speculations can be traced right down to the present day, and most clearly in certain 'philosophies of history' of which the Church emphatically disapproved. Horrified though the unworldly mystic would have been to see it happen, it is unmistakably the Joachite phantasy of the three ages that reappeared in, for instance, the theories of historical evolution expounded by the German Idealist philosophers Lessing, Schelling, Fichte, and to some extent Hegel; in Auguste Comte's idea of history as an ascent from the theological through the metaphysical up to the scientific phase; and again in the Marxian dialectic of the three stages of primitive communism, class society and final communism which is to be the realm of freedom and in which the state will have withered away.[26]

Thus, the intersection of the thought of Ficino, Pico, and Joachim has provided much of the framework of the modern world:

Hermeticism and Cabalist mysticism provided fifteenth-century thinkers with precisely such a framework within which Joachim's books obtained a new meaning. Renaissance concerns such as the expectation of an imminent 'Golden Age', the celebration of the human being as a terrestrial god, as a co-creator and *magus* who, through alchemy, magic and science, acts upon the world to shape it according to his liking, derived from the amalgamation of these three ingredients: Joachimism, Hermeticism and Cabalist mysticism. Their intersection marks the beginning of the modern epoch.[27]

---

seen as its supreme product." (*The Socialist Phenomenon*, trans. by William Tjalsma, [New York: Harper & Row, 1980] p. 130.)
26 Cohn, p. 109.
27 Stefan Rossbach, *Gnostic Wars—The Cold War in the Context of the History of Western Spirituality* (Edinburgh: Edinburgh University Press, 1999) p. 104.

It is this worldview, mingling immanentized eschatology, magic, Cabala, and Hermetical Gnosticism, which Hunnius confronts in his *Principia*.

### An Overview of the Structure of Hunnius' Principia

The structure of Hunnius' *Principia* is surprisingly complex, given the relative brevity of the work. Following a brief introduction, the remainder of the work is divided into five chapters which are, in turn, divided into various subpoints. In fact, it is relatively easy to become lost in the maze of subdivisions of the argument, if one is not familiar with the methodology of theological argumentation common to that era and a basic parallelism within the structure of the *Principia*.

While Hunnius' argumentation shows the careful attention to structure which is often rewarded with the charge of "scholasticism," his introduction of the work in question makes it clear that he understood his topic to be far removed from dry academic pursuit:

> So then, it was not enough Satanic madness to oppress the Church through the frenzy of the Antichrist, the deceits of Calvinism, and the tricks of Photinianism and in this way to sift the saints [Amos 9:9]; they also had to stir up some new breed, varied in its origin, hermaphroditic by profession, *alchemico-theological*, of pretended holiness, spiritual, united in essence with Christ, furnished with the direct inspiration of God and thus God-taught. For this reason, it was powerful in a profound knowledge of all things, with the ability of investigating the human heart, of foretelling the future, of interpreting Scripture, or performing miracles, and with the faculty of explaining whatever great thing has existed in the world. Finally, it overflowed with the riches of the entire world. Of these and other matters it boasts at great length in its published writings.

Hunnius believed the entirety of the fanatical theology to be permeated with "trifles" and "diabolic snares" (§II)—"a poisoned potion" mixed with "something quite pleasing" (§III). Hunnius' concern was that of a minister of the Word; the novelty of the Paracelsian/Weigelian doctrine is not something to be indulged, but "Satanic madness" to be openly opposed with all the means at his disposal. Contrary to the style of feigned ambivalence which has become quite common in academic writing today, Hunnius wrote as a steward of the mysteries of God, one who is "holding fast the faithful word as he has been taught, that he may be able, by sound doctrine, both to exhort and convict those who contradict." (Titus 1:9 NKJV)

In the first chapter ("On the origin and name of this sect."), Hunnius demonstrated a thorough knowledge of the origins of this doctrine and of the succession of teachers which led to the heresies of Paracelsus and Weigel:

> Comparatively speaking, he [Paracelsus] was the *primary* author, for we read of many authors who spread that poison, such as Albertus Magnus, H. Cornelius Agrippa, Aegidius of Rome, Gerhard of Sutphania, Johan Hagen de indagine, Johan Reuchlin, the Minorite Pietro Palatino, the Minorite Francisco Giorgio, Marsilio Ficino, William Postellus, Henry Horphius, Marco Antonio Mocenico, Stephan Conventanus. Some anonymous author relates to these the origin of cabalistic theology in the preface of his book *De Magia*. These men, I say, spread here and there the first seeds of their tares in the papist monasteries and schools, which were full of Satanic sorcery and diabolic arts, and they exerted themselves to infect their descendants with the rest of their writings. Paracelsus, however, used their works and by the productivity of his temperament, he sought out from them all their ideas with his eagerness for something new and stuffed his books with that material. In this way, those poisons

which we could have hoped would die along with the writings of the ancients were vindicated by his death and came into the hands especially of those who used those works in their eagerness to learn medicine. (§III)

Hunnius understood the connection of Paracelsian doctrine to a succession of teachers reaching back into the thirteenth century, and his understanding of the influence of figures such as Johann Reuchlin (the greatest proponent of Cabalistic studies in all of Germany), Marsilio Ficino (the father of the modern Hermeticism) and Cornelius Agrippa (made famous by his study of magic) is quite telling. So, too, he understood the connection between the Paracelsian doctrine and that of Reformation-era Enthusiasts: "At the same time, however, *Caspar Schwenkfeld, Carlstadt* and their associates, the *Anabaptists*, as well as other 'heavenly prophets,' each of whom drew something from the theology which was flowing into Paracelsus from one place or another, were producing their not dissimilar monster." (§V) Weigel, in turn, Hunnius recognized was not only shaped by these influences through Paracelsus, but was himself shaped by Ficino's most famous theologian of antiquity ("*Mercury Trismegistus*") and also by the mystics of the Medieval and Reformation eras: "Tauler... Dionysius ... and Thomas Müntzer" (§VII). And Hunnius connects the doctrine of Weigel to that of contemporary fanatics (Ezechiel Meth, and the Brotherhood of the Rosy Cross/Rosicrucians)—a theme which we will return to in our conclusion. By identifying the close theological kin of the Paracelsians and Weigelians, Hunnius established the place of such theology in the context of condemnations which are already to be found in the *Book of Concord*. For example, the twelfth article of the Formula of Concord condemns numerous articles of the Anabaptists which cannot be tolerated in the Church, the State, and the Home, and it condemns eight erroneous articles of the Schwenkfeldians. Luther's famous condemnation of Müntzer[28] in the Smalcald Articles sets the stage for condemning the Paracelsians and Weigelians for sharing Müntzer's contempt for the Scriptures. Much of the rest of the *Principia* is devoted to fleshing out the content of the fanatical traditions which Paracelsus and Weigel have received—and amplified.

The second chapter ("On the primary efficient cause of the theological institution, which the school of Paracelsus has rejected.") is, as its title indicates, dedicated to the fanatics' rejection of the Scripture as the only source of theology, and the effort of the fanatics to interpret Scripture according to their own private judgment. Hunnius thus set forth Holy Scripture as the norm of all theology: "That theology in which the principles as well as dogmas of faith and godliness are not sound and are not in harmony with the canon of Holy Scripture is not a divine theology." (§II) The express intention which permeates Hunnius' *Principia* is that which is set forth in Section II.I:

> The very satisfactory and, in fact, infallible criterion for recognizing the false prophets has been revealed to us in Mat. 7:15: *You will know them by their fruits*. As we pay attention to this, we seek those fruits not in some external appearance of saintliness, but we believe that those fruits exist chiefly in their doctrines of faith and godliness and in the principles thereof. Accordingly we in such wise accuse them of Paracelsic idle chatter.

---

28 "And in those things which concern the spoken, outward Word, we must firmly hold that God grants His Spirit or grace to no one, except through or with the preceding outward Word. Thereby we are protected against enthusiasts, i.e. spirits who boast that they have the Spirit without and before the Word, and accordingly judge Scripture or the spoken Word, and explain and stretch it at their pleasure, as Münzer did, and many still do at the present day; they wish to be acute judges between the Spirit and the letter, and yet know not what they say or propose." (SA III, VIII:3)

Hunnius maintained that the Paracelsians neglected the primary efficient cause by having disdain for the Word of God revealed in Holy Scripture; for Hunnius, "whoever in the business of faith does not bind himself entirely to Scripture does not hear as God teaches him, and overthrows the first foundation of sincere theology." (§XI) As for the Paracelsians, their theology "does not encourage the reading of the Bible but even disapproves of hearing it along with reading it." (§XIV) In place of the revealed word, the fanatics encourage their followers to learn the truth by examining their own hearts, based on the notion that all truth can be found within:

> The second effect is to *bestir that which lies in the heart* and to recall to memory that effect which Weigel appears to assign to Scripture. Indeed, from the fact that he does not even say this seriously and that on the basis of the hypothesis of the same school that Scripture does not even stir the mind in any way, it is obvious therefrom that the Paracelsists are awaiting a divine revelation, a momentary illumination, an internal discourse, a divine inspiration, an angelic conference—which remedies will remind them of those things which naturally lie hidden within hearts, according to that statement: *A person hears with the internal eye of his soul but considers the truth without any external persuasion* (*philos. mystic.*, p. 206).

Scripture, the fanatics maintain, "*has a double meaning and is ambigious*" (in Weigel's words) and he "ponders the serious mistake that the preachers and academics command their hearers to be content with the Word as that is preached from pulpits and commentaries on the Bible so that nothing is necessary to fly up into the heavens after the manner of the 'heavenly prophets' nor to await the illuminations of the Anabaptists." (§XXV) As for any meaning to be drawn from Scripture, the fanatics declare that "*the literal meaning is foreign to a Christian* as it comes forth from the old man, from the natural spirit of the world, from the Old Testament, from the Antichrist" (§XXXVI)—instead, it is necessary to bring meaning *to* Scripture (§XXXVIII).

Hunnius observed that the fanatics not only attack Scripture, but also those men who have been divinely called to proclaim God's Word. Hunnius maintains that to hear the "faithful pastors" is to "hear Christ teaching"; as for the Paracelsians, "They disrespect the successors of the apostles either as preachers or as writers and forbid people to listen to them, as they even now teach." By neglecting—even attacking—both the divinely inspired Word, and the ministry of that Word, the fanatic theology "does not permit the active principle of theological understanding to exist. As a consequence it rejects the true and primary cause of teaching." (§LIV)

As the second chapter addressed the Paracelsian/Weigelian rejection of the authority of Holy Scripture, and the office which Christ ordained for the proclamation of His Word, the third chapter turns to their rejection of the churches and schools in which that Word is proclaimed—the "organic and ordinary cause of theological instruction," as Hunnius termed it. Weigel declared ministers to be "mercenaries" (§VII) who lack that which he deemed necessary: an *immediate* call, and *immediate* divine instruction (§VIII), and such teachers must be sinless—a requirement which prompted Hunnius to retort, "If this is true, there will not be a single one of the mortal race who teaches theology fruitfully." (§XI) Not surprisingly, then, the fanatics "revile the churches because people bind themselves to them and torment themselves with the visiting of churches and listening to sermons" (§XIII), and they "curse vehemently the *academies* and their lecture halls as they claim that these are the enemies of Christ." (§XIV) The rejection of the preaching office is threefold, disparaging sermons (§XVI), "the reading of books" (§XVII), and "the exercises of debate" (§XVIII). All of this, Hunnius observed, was not because of "some abuse but also *per se.*" After all, Hunnius did not deny that there are abuses—immoral ministers, poor teachers, etc.—but the scandal of the fanatical theology is that it rejects the entirety of the office of the ministry and its work.

Having rejected both the substance of Christian theology (the doctrine revealed in Holy Scripture) and the means by which the theology is taught to the Church (the office of the ministry), upon what does Paracelsian theology rest? The fourth chapter is paired with the second chapter: if the fanatics have taken away the Word of God as the source of doctrine, what have they put in its place? Hunnius summarized their foundation at the beginning of chapter four:

> We find these foundations to be of two classes: some are *primary* and some *secondary*. We say that the former ones are, first, *the internal word which is innate in a person*; second, *divine revelation*; third, *the conversations of the angels*; fourth, *heavenly philosophy* which they pawn off as divine truth on the basis of, first, *the Cabala*; second, *astrology*; third, *alchemy*; and fourth, *mystic numbers*. (§II)

It is in chapter four that one begins to see more clearly the degree to which Hermeticism and Cabalistic studies have thoroughly permeated the entire theology of the fanatics. Hunnius devoted the chapter to refuting each of these foundations, demonstrating that each was utterly inadequate as a basis for sound teaching. Again and again, the emphasis in the *Principia* is on the inadequacy of such foundations to sustain faith and hope in the heart of believers; thus, for example, Hunnius noted regarding the inadequacy of natural revelation: "How shamefully, however, this begs the question and how dangerously they build faith on the sand (Mat. 7:26) and upon no rooted foundation we leave to each godly person for his upright investigation." (§VI) The notion that immediate inspiration can be relied upon as a source of doctrine was rejected by Hunnius, and he dismissed their purported conversation with angels with the argument that the testimony of Holy Scripture utterly opposes such a reliance. And Hunnius did not mask his open contempt for their reliance upon alchemy and the Cabala: "We justly wonder at that wisdom from beyond the sea because it scarcely appears that this comes forth from human talent, unless one's brain is attracted by the satanic arts." (§XXXIV)

The fifth chapter ("On a student's requirements which the school of Paracelsus prescribes for those who are learning") parallels the third chapter: If the fanatics have taken away the pastoral office and the regular call, what have they put in its place? Hunnius identified a three-fold abnegation on the part of the student which a Paracelsian teacher demands of him: (1) all worldly knowledge must be rejected, (2) the student can never argue with his teacher, and (3) the doctrine of *Gelassenheit* ("that abandonment of oneself" [§XXIII]), is required. In essence, the student is to utterly surrender himself to his teacher, offering no resistance at all to the new doctrine, and forsaking all biblical knowledge which he had acquired previously (§II), and even abandon his sense of self, so that he may be reshaped. Hunnius thus concluded his *Principia* with the declaration:

> We are agreed, however, on the basis of these very brief samplings, that *even the passive principle of theology*, that is, *the learner*, is transformed and corrupted in so ugly a fashion by the Paracelcists that he comes out as totally unsuitable for grasping theological instruction. From this there emerges the general conclusion:

## Therefore, the theology of Paracelsus is not divine.

This is what we had to prove.

The overt substitution of hidden doctrines, supposedly drawn from oneself, but which are imparted—without question—by the teacher who claims immediate inspiration is far removed from that Christian doctrine drawn from the divine Word and taught by those whom Christ has sent, mediately, to teach His Church.

However, by the time of the publication of Hunnius' *Principia* in 1619, the doctrine of the fanatics was already bringing havoc to the Church and State. As Frances Yates observed in her book, *The Rosicrucian Enlightenment*,[29] such a doctrine drove the decision of Frederick V, the elector Palatine, to initiate the chaos of the Thirty Years War by means of his willingness to accept the crown in Bohemia after the Defenestration of Prague. Already under the rule of Emperor Rudolph II, the city had become haven for the fanatics:

> [Rudolph II] moved the imperial court from Vienna to Prague, which became a centre for alchemical, astrological, magico-scientific studies of all kinds. Hiding himself in his great palace at Prague, with its libraries, its 'wonder rooms' of magico-mechanical marvels, Rudolph withdrew in alarm from the problems raised by the fanatical intolerance of his frightening nephew. Prague became a Mecca for those interested in esoteric and scientific studies from all over Europe. ... Jews might pursue their cabalistic studies undisturbed (Rudolph's favourite religious adviser was Pistorius, a Cabalist) and the native church of Bohemia was tolerated by an official 'Letter of Majesty.'[30]

When the new emperor, Ferdinand, brought all of this to an end with his rise to power, the Bohemian Brethren and those allied with them brought about a temporary change. The bordering Duchy of Württemberg was similarly inclined to support for mysticism, for "The alchemical and esoteric interests encouraged by Rudolph II had represented a more liberal, Renaissance atmosphere than that which the Reaction wished to impose, and such studies were popular at German courts,

---

29 (London and New York: Routledge, 1972).
30 ibid., p. 16–17.

particularly those of Hesse and Württemberg."[31] Indeed, the "Rosicrucian manifestos"—bearing the stamp of a theology influenced by the same teachers who shaped the doctrine of Paracelsus and Weigel—were written by an influential pastor of Württemberg, Johann Valentin Andreae.[32] The Joachimite expectations of the forces behind the short-lived reign of Frederick V—perhaps alluded to by Hunnius (4:XVII) and certainly very much in the minds of the men behind the Rosicrucian movement[33]—led to an overconfidence that victory was fated to the rebellion. Thus, in Yates' assessment:

> A culture was forming in the Palatinate which came straight out of the Renaissance but with more recent trends added, a culture which may be defined by the adjective 'Rosicrucian'. The prince around whom these deep currents were swirling was Frederick, Elector Palatine, and their exponents were hoping for a politico-religious expression of their aims in the movement towards the Bohemian adventure. As I begin to see it, all the mysterious movements of former years around such figures as Philip Sidney, John Dee, Giordano Bruno, were gathered to a head in the Anhalt propaganda for Frederick. The Frederickian movement was not the cause of these deep currents, and it was far from being the only expression of them. But it was an attempt to give those currents politico-religious expression, to realize the ideal of a Hermetic reform centred on a real prince. The movement tried to unite many hidden rivers in one stream, the Dee philosophy and the mystical chivalry from England were to join with German mystical currents. The new alchemy was to unite religious differences, and found a symbol in the 'chemical wedding' with its overtones of allusion to the 'mar-

---

[31] ibid., p. 27.
[32] Marshall rightly describes the manifestos as "strongly Hermetic and alchemical" (Peter Marshall, *The Magic Circle of Rudolf II*, [New York: Walker & Co., 2006] p. 234.)
[33] Yates, p. 35.

riage of the Thames and the Rhine'. We know that this movement was to fail disastrously, was to rush over a precipice into the abyss of the Thirty Years War.[34]

Thirty years of crushing warfare would be the lasting monument to the scale of the error.

As the war progressed, and Hunnius served as superintendent of Lübeck, he continued to combat the pernicious influence of the Paracelsian and Weigelian fanaticism. In Erdmann Rudolph Fischer's *The Life of John Gerhard*, a 1625 letter from Gerhard to Hunnius is preserved which offers a window into Hunnius' continued research. The letter deals with Johann Arndt (1555–1621), whose magnum opus, *True Christianity (de vero Christianismo)*, would prove to be the pivotal work inspiring the later Pietist movement, and in this letter, Gerhard addresses the influence of the fanatic theology on Arndt:

> I have known the aforementioned Arndt for many years because he was the bishop for several years in my home town. He has always professed to have a great and heartfelt interest in our [Augsburg] Confession and in the symbolical books of our churches and he has born public witness that we should understand his books according to their norm. I therefore cannot yet be persuaded to believe that some fanatic spirit has driven him to have confessed something with his lips but to have something else closed up in his heart, because he has always seemed to me to be a stranger to hypocrisy.
>
> Meanwhile, I do not deny that in his books *de vero Christianismo* there occur ambiguous phrases and, in fact, some of the type which one can draw easily into the meaning of Weigel. For this reason, when the very reverend and renowned prince and lord, Duke Christian of Brunswick and Luneberg, and the

---

34 Yates, p. 90.

bishop of Minden sent our faculty the Latin version of the four books *de vero Christianismo* and sought either their censure or approval, I responded along with my esteemed colleagues in this vein: that we were prepared to explain the things which appeared in Books 1, 2 and 4, although with the substitution of more appropriate phrasing and heading off any corruption, to the extent that we could do that; but that he had arranged Book 3 in such a way that one could scarcely correct it without the loss of a greater part thereof. For this reason, we refused our approval of the book. ... I think there are two reasons for his inappropriate and dangerous phrasing: the first, that he was especially given to the study of medicine in the academies and had not yet shaped his judgment about theological controversies by listening to lectures and holding discussions; but the second, that the reading of the books of Paracelsus and Weigel pleased him, for an eyewitness testifies that Arndt brought from them many things into his books *de vero Christianismo*.[35]

Modern analysis of Arndt has demonstrated that he incorporated even more of the 'fanatic theology' than Gerhard had realized into the writing of *True Christianity*.[36] And the influence of the 'fanatic theology' remained clearly present in the theology of Arndt's theological descendants, the Pietists.[37] Thus, for example, the basis of the thought of Friedrich Christoph Oetinger (1702-1782) is described as follows:
> The basis of his theological development rested on Lutheran Orthodoxy and piety; an intensified biblicism

---

35 E. R. Fischer, *The Life of John Gerhard*, trans. by Richard J. Dinda and Elmer Hohle, (Malone, Texas: Repristination Press, 2001) p. 425-426.
36 see Johannes Wallmann, "Johann Arndt" in *The Pietist Theologians—An Introduction to Theology in the Seventeenth and Eighteenth Centuries*, ed. by Carter Lindberg (Malden, Massachusetts: Blackwell Publishing, 2005) p. 30-31.
37 Peter C. Erb, *Pietists, Protestants, and Mysticism*, (Metuchen, New Jersey: The Scarecrow Press, 1989) p. 14.

and chiliasm mediated by Bengel; a greater nearness to the Old Testament, Judaism, and the Cabbala; a profound sympathy to hermeticism, neoplatonic images, and German philosophy of nature; and a deferential joy of discovery in nature, science, human individuality and society.[38]

The influence of the 'fanatic theology'—both as it was transmitted through the writings of Arndt and as it was absorbed by direct exposure to Hermeticism, Cabala, Paracelsian, and Weigelian theology—remains in need of further exploration in the history of the Pietist movement. Given the profoundly detrimental effects of the Thirty Years War and Pietism on the survival of Lutheran Orthodoxy, the fanatical theology condemned in the *Principia* may be rightly held to have been a significant factor in the decline of the Lutheran Church in the seventeenth and eighteenth centuries.

*Rt. Rev. James D. Heiser, M.Div., S.T.M.*
*The Festival of St. Matthias, Apostle, A.D. 2015*

---

38 Martin Weyer-Menkhoff, "Friedrich Christoph Oetinger" in *The Pietist Theologians—An Introduction to Theology in the Seventeenth and Eighteenth Centuries*, p. 250.

# PRINCIPIA THEOLOGIÆ FANATICÆ
## (*PRINCIPLES OF THE FANATIC THEOLOGY*)

WHICH THEOPHRASTUS PARACELSUS FATHERED,
WHICH WEIGEL POLISHED;

AS THESE WERE REDUCED UNDER EXAMINATION TO
BRIEF THESES

and
PRESENTED FOR SOLEMN DEBATE
WITH THE HELP OF GOD, THRICE *OPTIMUS MAXIMUS*,

by
**NICOLAUS HUNNIUS**,
DOCTOR OF THEOLOGY AND PUBLIC PROFESSOR,
AS HE RESPONDED

to
M. VALENTINUS LEGDAEUS OF
SUERINUM-MEGAPOLITANUM
WHO WAS SEEKING TO OBTAIN THE HIGHEST GRADE
OF THEOLOGY

on
THE SEVENTH DAY OF MAY
DURING THE MORNING AND AFTERNOON HOURS
IN HIS THEOLOGICAL EXAMINATION

The heirs of Johann Richter printed these
at Wittenberg in the year 1619

## I

[1][1] So then, it was not enough Satanic madness to oppress the Church through the frenzy of the Antichrist, the deceits of Calvinism, and the tricks of Photinianism and in this way to sift the saints [Amos 9:9]; they also had to stir up some new breed, varied in its origin, hermaphroditic by profession, *alchemico-theological*,[2] of pretended holiness, spiritual, united in essence with Christ,[3] furnished with the direct inspiration of God and thus God-taught[4]. For this reason, it was powerful in a profound knowledge of all things, with the ability of investigating the human heart, of foretelling the future, of interpreting Scripture, or performing miracles, and with the faculty of explaining whatever great thing has existed in the world. Finally, it overflowed with the riches of the entire world. Of these and other matters it boasts at great length in its published writings.

## II

Each prudent person readily detects these trifles of the fanatics and the diabolic snares they have prepared to deceive wretched mortals and which they have cloaked with an attractive appearance of holiness. This is not so easy for the more naive.

## III

As those who offer a poisoned potion to others mix something quite pleasing in the same drink to conceal the hostile assault of the potion by covering it with sweetness, so in no lesser fashion do those [fanatics] have the appearance of godliness, however much they may deny its virtue as their public writings speak, although those writings make a great noise with their many errors.

---

1 Pagination on the 1619 text is thus indicated throughout this edition.
2 Use of italics in this text largely conforms to the usage of the 1619 text.
3 *cum Christo essentialiter unita*
4 θεοδιδάκτους

## IV

Because here they are not peddling their saintliness as much as that sect reveals it, they are not only commending the art of alchemy but are in this way sprinkling their ugly errors throughout all the articles of faith and practicing all heresies. For this reason, it has seemed worthwhile to reveal now at least some specimen of that monstrous "theology" and to show upon what *principles* they have founded it.

## V

[2a] While we are attempting to do this with the good help of God, we ourselves say in general with that prophetic utterance: *To the Law and to the testimony! If they do not speak according to this word, they will not have the morning light.* [Isa. 8:8] Let the Word be the norm and only rule outside of which we hold nothing as divine, nothing as godly, nothing as sacred.

## VI

Furthermore, we are not giving this purpose as intended through our own powers. The truth does not lie within us—our every thought is wicked, we stray on our own ways which are not good ones, unless the Word of the Lord be a lamp for our feet and a light for our paths, [Psa. 119:105] and He who is the truth and who cannot lie teach us those things which are salutary. Accordingly, O Father of lights, we invoke you in spirit and in truth; and You, O Son of the Father and the *Logos*, who has revealed the will of God; and You, O Holy Spirit, who lead people into all truth: fill our hearts with Your heavenly light, grant us understanding that we deal with Your Word in pious and holy fashion. May we bring no [human] meaning upon it, may we add nothing thereto, take nothing therefrom. Let us find in it the truth which we are seeking with godly mind and sincere heart. May we dispel successfully the fog of falseness with which fanatic theology dazzles[5] the eyes of the naive. May we detect its errors to the glory of Your most holy name, to the growth and increase of the Church, and finally to our salvation and to that of others. Amen.

---

5 *perstringit*

# CHAPTER I
## On the origin and name of this sect.

I

We follow the custom of the Church of all time and ascribe to the sect the name *"Paracelsic"* from, if not its first creator, certainly its primary creator, whose name we know today as *Theophrastus Paracelsus*,[6] a quite renowned physician of the previous century.

II

We do not envy this man for the praise he enjoyed—if he deserved such in his skills—nor do we wish to harm or remove from him in any way such praise as we bear our witness about him. [3] We are now involved in a theological forum which makes clear that this man is one of scarcely any trustworthiness and otherwise of a shameful life, and that he is the sort of fanatic worse than almost any other of whom we read. This is not to mention the diabolic magic[7] which, if it does not convict him, certainly makes him most suspicious. All those works of his which are publicly extant and which a Christian person reads with astonishment and surprise bear more than sufficient testimony.

---

6 Theophrastus Bombastus von Hohenheim took the name "Paracelsus," though there remains debate regarding the intention behind this action; as Andrew Weeks observes, "the root intention of the name *Paracelsus*—a name that appeared on tracts ushered into print in the author's lifetime—has not been resolved to the agreement of scholars. It is either an oblique rendering of Hohenheim, or perhaps a boast that the so-named exceeds the ancient medical authority Celsus, or that the bearer is the author of works of a paradoxical, antithetical character." (*Paracelsus—Speculative Theory and the Crisis of the Early Reformation*, [Albany: State University of New York Press, 1997] p. 3.)

7 *magiam diobolicam*

## III

Comparatively speaking, he was the *primary* author, for we read of many authors who spread that poison, such as Albertus Magnus,[8] H. Cornelius Agrippa,[9] Aegidius of Rome,[10] Gerhard of Sutphania,[11] Johan Hagen de indagine,[12] Johan Reuchlin,[13] the Minorite Pietro Palatino,[14] the Minorite Francisco Giorgio,[15] Marsilio Ficino,[16] William Postellus,[17]

---

8  Albertus Magnus (1193–1280), medieval theologian and philosopher, who was the teacher of Thomas Aquinas. He was deeply interested in astrology, and was reputed to have an interest in alchemy, though much of the literature which is attributed to him in that field is pseudepigraphical in nature.

9  Heinrich Cornelius Agrippa (1486–1535) lectured at the University of Dole in 1512 on Reuchlin's *De verbo mirifico*. He was the author of a major work in the realm of occult literature, *De occulta philosophia libri tres*.

10  i.e., Aegidius of Viterbo (1469–1532), an Italian Augustinian who was made a Cardinal by Pope Leo X. Aegidius was a Cabalist, and had been a student of Marsilio Ficino and Giovanni Pico della Mirandola at Florence.

11  i.e., Gerard Zerbolt (1367–1398), a Dutch mystical writer and member of the Brothers of the Common Life. *De spiritualibus ascensionibus* is among his works.

12  Johannes Indagine (1467–1537), a Carthusian, and German astronomer. He was apparently also an advocate of chiromancy, which purports to tell the future by means of the study of the human palm.

13  Johannes Reuchlin (1455–1522), a student of Marsilio Ficino and Giovanni Pico della Mirandola who introduced Cabalistic studies north of the Alps. His most famous work of Cabala, *De Arte Cabalistica*, was dedicated to Pope Leo X. Reuchlin was the uncle of Lutheran reformer Philipp Melanchthon.

14  i.e., Peter Abelard (1079–1142), accused of holding a rationalistic interpretation of the docrine of the Trinity.

15  i.e., Francesco Giorgi Veneto (1466–1540), a Franciscan friar and Cabalist from Venice. He wrote *De harmonia mundi totius cantica tria* (1525) and *In Scripturam Sacram Problemata* (1536). He is considered a synthesizer of the thought of Ficino and Pico.

16  Neo-Platonist and Hermeticist, Ficino (1433–1499) was the founder of the Platonic Academy in Florence and canon of the cathedral in that city. Throughout his writings, Ficino advocated the viewpoint that the ancient pagan religious were also divinely-established, and that they were recipients of divine revelations in their various holy books, oracles, etc.

17  Postellus was a member of the Jesuits for a time but was dismissed for his heretical views and imprisoned by the Inquisition. He escaped to France and was favorably received by King Charles IX. His books (which include *De Trinitate, De Matrice Mundi, De Omnibus Sectis salvandis, De future Nativitate Mediatoris*) have been described as "filled with the most extravagant of errors" (Alphonsus M. Liguori). Postellus died in 1581. Among other oddities, it is purported that Postellus had claimed that women

Henry Horphius, Marco Antonio Mocenico,[18] Stephan Conventanus. Some anonymous author relates to these the origin of cabalistic theology in the preface of his book *De Magia*.[19] These men, I say, spread here and there the first seeds of their tares in the papist monasteries and schools, which were full of Satanic sorcery and diabolic arts, and they exerted themselves to infect their descendants with the rest of their writings. Paracelsus, however, used their works and by the productivity of his temperament, he sought out from them all their ideas with his eagerness for something new and stuffed his books with that material. In this way, those poisons which we could have hoped would die along with the writings of the ancients were vindicated by his death and came into the hands especially of those who used those works in their eagerness to learn medicine.

## IV

While Theophrastus was among the living, he did not dare promote in the bosom of the Church his pregnant theological warfare to which he was giving birth, and this is a sign of his bad conscience, although we hear that he was in the habit of saying frequently that he was *going to reform at some time Luther and Melanchthon in no other way than as he did in the cases of Galen and Hippocrates in medicine*.

## V

At the same time, however, *Caspar Schwenkfeld*,[20] *Carlstadt* and their associates, the *Anabaptists*, as well as other "heavenly prophets," each of whom drew something from the theology which was flowing into Paracelsus from one place or another, were producing their not dissimilar monster. [4]

---

would need a female savior.
18  i.e., Marco Antonio Mocenigo, who was bishop of Ceneda, Italy from 1586–1598. He wrote *De anima eiusque divinum ad Deum Raptu* (1581) and *de transitu hominis ad deum* (1586).
19  Perhaps a reference to *Arbatel de magia veterum*, an anonymous work first published in 1575 in Basel, Switzerland.
20  Schwenkfeld (1489–1561), rejected infant baptism and the real presence in the Lord's Supper. In his *Great Confession*, he maintained that Jesus human nature was a celestial flesh which was undergoing a progressive deification, becoming more divine.

## VI

The divine goodness of Luther and (in the years following) that of other good men put to rest with their ministry those burning flames so that only tiny remnants thereof survived until some fellow of otherwise undistinguished name—M. Valentin Weigel[21]—brought them back to life. His writings (which originated thirty years earlier) are being printed by badly-motivated people with the work of hungry or greedy typographers—but without naming the place and printshop of their printing and not without peril to the state of the Church. That is also resulting in the present damage to the Church in these years close to our time. We agree, too, that we have some quite clear suspicion that under the name of Weigel (as also of Paracelsus) other supporters of their errors are crafting new pamphlets therefrom.

## VII

We do not tarry over the fact that Weigel connects some other manufacturers and patriarchs of his theology to Theophrastus, some of whom are renowned and some undistinguished, like *Mercury* [Hermes] *Trismegistus*[22] (*post.*[23], part 2, p. 39 and 263; *gülden Griff*[24], p. 52); [Johann]

---

21 Weigel (1533–1588) was influenced by the writings of Paracelsus and Schwenkfeld. Although a Lutheran pastor from 1567, he privately dissented from the Formula of Concord, even though he publicly subscribed it. His mystical writings were largely undertaken in private and only became widely known after his death.

22 The 'Hermetic'/Gnostic attributed to Hermes Trismegistus were translated and published by Marsilio Ficino in the late 15th century. Many of the adherents of the Hermetic doctrines believed Hermes to be a contemporary of Moses who was a recipient of a divine revelation—a pagan Gospel—given for the salvation of the Gentiles. Ficino viewed him as one of the *prisci theologi*—the 'ancient theologians'—who were divinely inspired, and formed a succession from Zoroaster to Plato.

23 The work entitled *Postilla—Sermons—*is abbreviated in a variety of ways by Hunnius. In modern Weigelian literature it is commonly referred to as the *Manuscript Collection of Sermons*, and is believed to have been composed between November 1573 and March 1574. (*Valentin Weigel—Selected Spiritual Writings*, trans. by Andrew Weeks, [New York: Paulist Press, 2003] p. 40.)

24 A modern English translation of Weigel's *gülden Griff—The Golden Grasp* (1578)—has been published in *Valentin Weigel—Selected Spiritual Writings*.

*Tauler*[25] (part 2, *post.*, p. 87 and 104; *gülden Griff*, p.43); *Dionysius*[26] (*post.*, part 2, p. 104; *theologus de morte, post,* part 2, p. 303; *Lautensach,* part 3, *post.,* p. 96); and Thomas Müntzer[27] (*dialog. de Christian.,* p. 8 and 52). Theophrastus towers over all these. Here he has gathered many things of which others have gathered a few things here and there and have dealt with quite obscurely but he more clearly. He has also reduced all of these matters into a single chaos with greater success than have any of the rest. It is under this name that we relate Weigelian theology to Paracelsus as the director of the fanatics of this time.

## VIII

It is not enough that in the years just passed some fellow Ezechiel Meth[28] eagerly performed not a little work in the neighboring churches. He had been reared in the school of Paracelsus and to some extent brought into light the theology of Paracelsus, although, when Meth received a stern admonition, he condemned the errors of his teacher. He later returned to the vomit of the latter, however. The Brotherhood of the Rosy Cross[29] [Rosicrucians] immediately joined Meth, having promised mountains of gold to themselves and others who were going to profess their own names to that brotherhood and this without memoranda, scarcely a handful of which exist. The more experienced interpret with a definite suspicion [5] this fraternity as utopian, and its writings as the products of idle brethren and of shameless temperaments. If this is the case, we grieve with sincere heart that we have discovered this devilish deceit that they know how to prepare, through peddlers of finery, snares for the more naive and twist the target of their faith.

25 Johann Tauler (1360–1361), a German mystic.
26 Pseudo-Dionysius the Areopagite. The 6th century *Corpus Areopagiticum* includes several mystical works which demonstrate clear Neo-Platonic influences.
27 Müntzer (1489–1525), a violent Anabaptist theologian who was involved in provoking and leading the peasants during the rebellion of 1524–25. Müntzer was executed after the Battle of Frankenhausen.
28 Ezechiel Meth (†1640), like his uncle, the Thuringian spiritualist, Esaias Stiefel (†1627), rejected the written Word of Scripture and the Sacraments. He was reconciled to the Lutheran Church before his death.
29 *fraternitas roseæ crucis*

## IX

Moreover, these, whoever they may be, as well as others who are excessively puffed up, all acknowledge *Theophrastus* as their father, and because we could scarcely have doubted this with regard to the rest, *Weigel*, who otherwise did not openly pursue the practice of medicine, sends his readers back to *Paracelsus* as to a man divinely illumined (*post.*, part 1, p. 195; part 2, p. 257 and 266; part 3, p. 96, *gülden Griff*, p. 20, 48, 49 and 52; *libell. disputat.*[30], p. 26, 28, 29 and 42). The descendants of Weigel should connect this father of theirs with Theophrastus in such a way that they publish several writings of both and put those writings into a single volume with the title *Philosophia Mystica*. In this way, the conformity of their dogmas say this very thing, as a comparison thereof proves.

---

30  Weigel's *Libellus Disputatorius* was published in 1618; as Weigel scholar Andrew Weeks observes, the *Libellus'* opposition to basing "just war" arguments on Old Testament texts does "much to account for the reputation of 'Weigelianism' during the Thirty Years' War." (*Valentin Weigel—German Religious Dissenter, Speculative Theorist, and Advocate of Tolerance*, [Albany: State University of New York Press, 2000] p. 182.)

## CHAPTER II
### On the primary efficient cause of the theological institution, which the school of Paracelsus has rejected.

I

The very satisfactory and, in fact, infallible criterion for recognizing the false prophets has been revealed to us in Mat. 7:15: *You will know them by their fruits.* As we pay attention to this, we seek those fruits not in some external appearance of saintliness, but we believe that those fruits exist chiefly in their doctrines of faith and godliness and in the principles thereof. Accordingly we in such wise accuse them of Paracelsic idle chatter.

II

That theology in which the principles as well as dogmas of faith and godliness are not sound and are not in harmony with the canon of Holy Scripture is not a divine theology.[31] [6]

III

Indeed, this proposition whose foundation lies in the midst of a quite sound theology rests upon the first principal thereof, namely, that it is the Law and the testimony. In this way, it justly holds the position of a principle and demands no further proof.

---

31 Throughout the translation, the use of a larger font to emphasize key points will reflect the usage of the 1619 original text.

## IV

**Such is the theology of Paracelsus**, that it contains the muscle that judges our proof and entire investigation and therefore must receive confirmation. We shall arrange the doing of this in such a way that, above all, we examine both his principles as well as those of true theology and compare them with each other.

## V

PRINCIPLES are either true or false. We call those *true* which God has commended to us as principles in which we must find saving truth and which we must observe scrupulously. Those are *false* which the heterodox establish for themselves despite the fact that God either has never prescribed them as those which we must follow, or which He has even commanded us to be wary of [them].

## VI

As a result, this proof has two parts. Whatever theology, first, disapproves of those true principles of faith and religion which God has commended; and second, on the contrary, whatever theology rests upon alien matters which people have invented and of which God has not approved and has at times forbidden; I say, such theologies are not divine and sound. We place the theology of Paracelsus under both parts not without the power of proofs.

## VII

**First, the theology of Parcelsus rejects divinely-proved principles.** The explanation and confirmation of it commands one to give his attention equally to the teacher and to the learner, for they then advance in instruction[32] when both behave correctly.

---

32 *doctrina*

## VIII

At one time, God taught the ancient fathers in many and different ways through His mercy seat (Exo. 25:21); through the linen ephod (1 Sam. 23:9), or the Urim and Thummin of the priest (1 Sam. 23:9ff, and 30:7, and Exo. 28:30); through His assumed human form (Gen. 18:2, etc.); through His appearances [7] (Isa. 6:1, Eze. 1:26, Exo. 24:10 and 3:2); through visions (Gen. 28:12 and 13; Jer. 1, 11 and 13; Zec. 1:8, 18 and 21); through conversations in dreams (Gen. 20:3, Num. 12:6 and 22:20); and through speaking face to face (Exo. 38:11).

## IX

In the New Testament, God has spoken to us in His Son (Heb. 1:1), who is the *Logos* of the Father and has told things which have neither been seen nor heard (John 1:18). Because He no longer speaks to us directly, He has set up His ministers as well as His apostles, prophets, pastors and teachers to gather the Church for Him on earth, to build up His spiritual body (Eph. 4:11), not by applying dogmas of wisdom made up from their own talents, but which conform to the norm of the Word which the prophets and apostles have prescribed, which Word therefore is renowned as the foundation of the Church (Eph. 2:20). In this way, that Word teaches the Church either in public assembly and meeting ordinarily, or privately in season or out of season (2 Tim. 4:2), or it teaches that letter orally or by letter (2 The. 2:15), that is, by speaking or with the living voice, but which now has been written.

## X

Therefore, we must consider the primary teachers: first, GOD; second, CHRIST, by reason of His special office.

## XI

First, inasmuch therefore as GOD no longer uses direct appearances and inspirations (as the following pages will teach), He has revealed His own will in the words which the prophets and apostles have written, and He has commanded us to learn that will from their writings (John 5:39, Luke 16:29 and 30; and Isa. 8:20), as that will is included therein sufficiently and clearly (2 Tim. 3:15ff.), and is infallibly true.[33] Whoever wishes to have God as his teacher pays attention to this word (2 Pet. 1:19). However, whoever holds it in contempt does not see the light of divine truth (Isa. 8:10). From this, then, we form the following proposition: **Whoever in the business of faith does not bind himself entirely to Scripture does not hear as God teaches him, and overthrows the first foundation of sincere theology.** [8]

## XII

We subsume *that the theology of Paracelsus does not bind itself totally to Scripture*. We prove this, in that he does not set it upon the foundation of dogmas, nor on the interpretation of the Word. As a result, we are agreed, *first*:

## XIII

1. *That his theology sets forth for mortals as many dogmas as possible for them to believe, which dogmas are not in Scripture nor are they drawn therefrom*. If you demand examples, I shall give you a few of them from the many available, lest the list grow excessively. Solely from the *philosophia mystica*, it holds the following: GOD *created man and did this out of NOTHING* (philos. myst., p. 138); *every creature and human being had both good and evil before the fall* (ibid., p. 139); *He created angels that they might be like God* (p. 208, 220 and 141); *being born again is failing by oneself, hating and denying oneself, dying to oneself, forgetting oneself and all his powers, etc.* (p. 145 and 146); *through regeneration, a human becomes God and God human* (p. 146, 172 and 188); *God is the essence of all things just as the alphabet is the essence of all syllables and words* (p.149); *before creation, God is without work, without emotion, without person - wircklosz, affectlosz und personlosz* (p.156 and 157); *the book is internal* [i.e., in man] *in which all things, divine and human, have been written, etc.* (p.157); *an angel can be everywhere* (p.168); *evil spirits*

---

33 *infallibiliter verum est*

*are forced into four elements* (p. 170 and 209); *God and souls are of the same nature* (p. 171); *the exiling from Paradise is not by reason of place but by reason of a voluntary turning away therefrom* (p. 172); *being born again is a property of infants alone* (p. 173); *after the universal end, the bodies of neither the blessed nor of the condemned will be present* (p. 175); *the body of Christ is supernatural, lacking every element and anything composed of elements, light-giving, spiritual and deified* (p. 175); *mortal and Adamitic flesh and blood will not inherit the kingdom of heaven; the flesh must be from Christ; it must be incorruptible and celestial flesh, incarnate by the Holy Spirit* (p. 175); *not God nor the angels nor the blessed accomplish anything because there is no need for those* (p.177). *Nothing external grants salvation regardless of under what name it may come* (p. 184); *in man after the fall there is good, namely, spiritual good* (p. 203); *the letter or the Word of Scripture is of no external operation* (p. 205); *the external Adamitic human comes into neither hell nor heaven, he is consumed by the elements and is saved or condemned internally alone* (p. 206); *the Word of God, Christ, and His kingdom* [9] *are infused from outside by a bare operation, and, if they are not essential to us, all sermons will be useless to us* (p. 206); *Christ will cease to exist according to His flesh* (p. 221); *Adam was staying in the Son before the Fall* (p. 222); *There are two Christs: the external one who was the son of Mary, and the internal one who dwells in the heart of the godly* (p. 223). These have not been drawn from Scripture, nor have we seen a single letter to offer its witness to these dogmas.

## XIV

2. *We agree that this theology does not encourage the reading of the Bible but even disapproves of hearing it along with reading it.* It is not without deceit that a Christian person is sent back to the Word of God in the school of Paracelsus as often as it commends the Word of God, as Weigel says (part 1, *post.*, p.49), because this means nothing else to Christians than the prophetic and apostolic *writing*. The Paracelsists, however, take that [Word of God] to mean writing which has been inspired by *any private and immediate inbreathing*.

## XV

You will not hear easily an encouragement to *read* Scripture. "Scripture" is being applied with a double usage here: first, through the eyes, and the *reading* of it is commended uniquely to us in 1 Tim. 4:13, Deu. 17:19 and 31:11, and Isa. 34:18; second, we also *hear* it through our ears, and we have a frequent command about this, as in Luke 16:29, etc. In both instances we need a godly attention (John 5:39).

## XVI

In addition, you will see that this theology disapproves quite often of the *hearing* of Scripture. In fact, the reason is obvious, for, because it is *useless, superfluous*, lacks virtue, is a dead letter and has no power to strike and move hearts (Weigel, *post.*, part 2, p. 225). [According to the Paracelsists:] you surely use this hearing in vain and in no other way than if you were to pick up the poems of Ovid to read for this reason—that you be enlightened thereby for eternal salvation.

## XVII

For this reason, we argue that every operating or active principle of theology works something in its subject. Scripture works nothing in shaping a person. Therefore Scripture is not an active principle of theology.

## XVIII

We prove the minor premise in this way. We can assign two effects to the reading of Scripture, one of which is to *teach*. The descendants of Paracelsus are unaware of this, as they affirm that [10] all knowledge lies hidden within the human heart so that one learns absolutely nothing inside by reading or hearing Scripture, but that all things already known are revealed to him by drawing it in from outside. This is something that Weigel separates in detail (*libell. disput.*). Take these themes from this pamphlet as well as from his other writings: *Something from the outside does not produce interior results; external things do not accomplish internal ones* (p. 12). *We seek understanding from a heart illuminated from within, not from a book* (p. 18). *All knowledge of divine matters comes from within and not from books* (*gülden Griff*, p. 8 and 9). *The apostles teach and write nothing else but that very thing which lies within us* (*post.*, part 2, p. 303). *We do not seek understanding from the Bible* (p. 14), *Know yourself* (part 1, p. 73). And the *summa: Faith can exist without external hearing* (*post.*, part 2, p. 234 and 235). Also: *A person can have knowledge and understanding even without Scripture* (*libell. disput.*, p. 19). *Scripture is an external mirror which indicates to you what is beautiful or ugly, sick or healthy, but it does not cause and cannot heal or ease your illnesses nor pains* (*gülden Griff*, p. 59). We find similar statements in Theophrastus (*labyr. medic.*, c. 8, Vol. 2, p. 174, Basel edition in quarto, of the year 1589).

## XIX

I conclude the following [regarding this theology]: there is no purpose nor use for Holy Scripture whether read or predicated.

## XX

The second effect is to *bestir that which lies in the heart* and to recall to memory that effect which Weigel appears to assign to Scripture. Indeed, from the fact that he does not even say this seriously and that on the basis of the hypothesis of the same school, Scripture does not even stir the mind in any way, it is obvious therefrom that the Paracelsists are awaiting a divine revelation, a momentary illumination, an internal discourse, a divine inspiration, an angelic conference—which remedies will remind them of those things which naturally lie hidden within hearts, according to that statement: *A person hears with the internal eye of his soul but considers the truth without any external persuasion* (*philos. mystic.*, p. 206). What, then, does Scripture do—especially since to him it is an empty and dead letter that stays on the paper, the bare testimony of that which a person not only has in his heart but also remembers well, as the Holy Spirit suggests this to him internally? (*post.*, part 2, p. 240 and part 3, p. 19, and [11] *dialog. de Christ.*, p.29 and 32.) We should note especially that among the requirements of a pupil in the school of Paracelsus, this too is claimed, that man abandons Scripture: *"Ein recht gelassen Mensch musz die H. Schrifft gelassen"*; and that a person does not have to know the letter but how to enter into the virtue of the Lord, etc. (Weigel, *von der gelassenheit*, p. 17). They themselves should have seen how that stands along with their remembrance.

## XXII

Again, however, we know that our handling of Scripture is in vain and of no effect, just as if I were to persuade you very laboriously to read some book from which you clearly would learn nothing but which nevertheless would teach only matters which you already knew and which you meet anywhere—the whiteness of snow, the changing of nights and days, the heat of fire, the light of the sun, and many more similar things which you already knew sufficiently before.

## XXIII

It is not that which they accept, that Scripture recalls into our mind and memory those things which had first been hiding in one's heart whether asleep or dead and that it does not lack its own necessary use. Although they may admit generally that the sciences are stirred by the reading of books through recalling and remembering, nevertheless with reference to sacred literature we will find that they scarcely affirm this. Even if we do find it, they again overturn this with their second theme (by which they contend that this happens through the immediate inspiration of God made under a sabbatical silence, which we shall speak about later).

## XXIV

3. *We agree that this theology judges that Scripture to be completely inappropriate for theological information.* We show this in the following way. Whatever [first,] may have two meanings and is ambiguous, second, whatever offers its support to all, regardless of how serious an error

they are making; third, which offers no help to those who are in agony; fourth, which is used in ridiculous fashion in elevating faith in the case of the death of neighbors; fifth, which is subject to vanity; sixth, which is imperfect; seventh, which does not shape a definite judgment about faith; I say, whatever is like this is inappropriate for the shaping of theology, and thus is not a true principle of theology.

## XXV

However, on the basis of the hypothesis of Paracelsus: Holy Scripture (1) *has a double meaning and is ambiguous*. Weigel (*post.*, part 2, p. 185): "Scripture is ambidextrous. Scripture is in both hands, although we may use it in one part. [12] Although someone may err, nevertheless he can oppose Scripture to his adversary" (*gülden Griff.*, p. 55). "Scripture is a two-handed letter. Someone may use it in any way he wishes, and for this reason very many sects and schisms exist," and this he also repeats in many words (p. 58). (2) *It supports everyone, regardless of how seriously he may err*. These passages just listed prove [this to be the doctrine of the Paracelsists]. (3) *It provides no help for those who are in agony*. It is very clear that the Paracelsists claim this, for Weigel ridicules facetiously those who collect and defend statements of the Bible with their debates, readings, discourses, etc. (*von der gelassenheit*, p. 7). (4) *People use it ridiculously to build up faith in the case of the death of neighbors*. "Here the priest or Scripture is of no help in my distress; neither confession nor the Sacraments help me in my anguish" (*dialog. de Christ.*, p. 88 and 117). "It introduces a guest who is near death, but the priest cannot help him with statements from Scripture. Rather, the priest (says) that he will comfort him with elegant statements taken from Scripture that the dying person recall more often the death of Christ." (5) *Scripture is subject to vanity*. "Anyone can use Scripture according to his own good pleasure, because the creature is subject to vanity" (*güld Griff.*, p. 58). (6) *It is imperfect*. Weigel (*dialog.*, p. 8) ponders the serious mistake that the preachers and academics command their hearers to be content with the Word as that is preached from pulpits and commentaries on the Bible so that nothing is necessary to fly up into the heavens after the manner of the "heavenly prophets" nor to await the illuminations of the Anabaptists.

He thinks, then, that neither Scripture nor sermons are enough for the Christian person to fly into heaven and await from Scripture revelations. (7) *Scripture does not shape a specific judgment regarding faith.* This is clear from the fact that it reveals the second part. You see, if Scripture holds true for both sides of litigants and offers its support to both, it surely does not teach the sort of judgment through which one party gives up and the other understands that it has won the case.

## XXVI

Therefore, according to the hypothesis of Paracelsus, Scripture is inappropriate for the outlining of theology.

## XXVII

4. *We agree with this,*[34] *because it opposes Scripture to theological truth.* Paracelsus considers as theological truth whatever the light of nature or heavenly revelation may have dictated. That Scripture is very much opposed to this [notion] will become clear [13] to the person who has examined dictates of this kind according to Holy Writ. When he commends his magical art,[35] Theophrastus (Bk.5, *de orig. morb. invisib.*, p. 316) bears with difficulty the fact that Scripture designates the Egyptian magicians with very harsh names, and adds: "This does not depend on the names, for the art can give the names a different meaning." A little later he affirms that God and nature developed that diabolic art.

## XXVIII

From this, we conclude as follows. Whoever makes Scripture a dead letter, powerless to convert a person, which does not teach nor cause one to remember things he knew before and claims that it is completely inappropriate for forming of theology; I say, such a person opposes theological truth, does not and cannot encourage the reading of the Bible, and consequently, does not bind himself totally to Scripture.

---

34 ie., the thesis *"that the theology of Paracelsus does not bind itself totally to Scripture."* See ❰XII above.

35 *artem magicam*

However, the theology of Paracelsus is like this, as we have demonstrated. In this way, we have proved that the theology of Paracelsus is not bound to Holy Writ *in the planting and strengthening of dogmas.*

## XXIX

Next, we are correct in asserting the same thing concerning the *interpretation* of Scripture, first, in that it [the Paracelsian theology] completely rejects what we have sought from Scripture; second, that it proves solely that which is brought and attached to it from other sources, etc.; and third, that it disapproves the method of true interpretation.

## XXX

We are sure that Holy Writ sets the theological foundation and that the principal question raised concerns the real meaning which one infers, that he who presumes to fault Scripture in his interpretation removes all Scripture.

## XXXI

On the other hand, we conclude that this finally is the true interpretation which follows closely the meaning of the Holy Spirit and which says nothing else but what the Holy Spirit wants to say and wants us to understand. That we may follow this, then, these canons show us, first, *No prophetic Scripture is of one's own interpretation* (2 Pet. 1:20); second, *that all interpretation must be according to the analogy of faith* (Rom. 12:6); third, *that the Word must be taught in a direct way* (2 Tim. 2:15). For this reason, we set up three general principles for the true interpretation of Scripture. First, *we should bring no meaning to the Biblical text* [from ourselves or from outside]. Second, *we must take every meaning and the harmony of Scripture from the very text.* Third, *we must organize and arrange the interpretation.* [14]

## XXXII

On the basis of these principles, we argue in this way: Whoever (1) rejects the interpretation drawn from Scripture and (2) commends only that interpretation brought to the text from an outside source and, (3) disapproves the true method of interpretation—such a person is not bound to Scripture in his interpretation. We subsume the following:

## XXXIII

First, *the theology of Theophrastus rejects the interpretation drawn from Scripture*. This is obvious in the fact that it very seriously injures the *literal* sense thereof which flows of itself and directly from Scripture and which alone is infallible[36].

## XXXIV

No godly person can doubt that the Holy Spirit—as the absolutely faithful Teacher of the Church—wanted the matters of which He wrote to be understood in just the way as the letters sound and the nature of the text bears, or destined the individual texts to the signifying of some specific perception, and that He did not write in such a way that anyone might add to it a mystic meaning[37] according to his own judgment.

## XXXV

We are not saying that the *literal* meaning is the first and direct meaning[38] of the words and phrases taken grammatically, but that meaning which the words can provide of themselves and first just as they are used in the text, for the literal meaning in those words of Isaiah (11:6): *The wolf will dwell with the lamb*, explains the union not of those beasts but of the Gentiles and the Jews.

---

36 *solus etiam infallibilis est*
37 *mysticum sensum*
38 *primum & immediatum*

## XXXVI

It is one thing, however, to elicit from the same text after the literal meaning also other meanings through it, under the guidance of Scripture, but it is another to reject the literal meaning entirely and bring in only spiritual meanings made up according to one's good pleasure, which, although it deserves rejection, nevertheless Paracelsus frequently commits with his idle chatter when he refers to the *literal meaning*.[39]

## XXXVII

(1) *He judges that the literal meaning is foreign to a Christian* as it comes forth from the old man, from the natural spirit of the world, from the Old Testament, from the Antichrist. (See Weigel, *dialog.*, p. 81; the *libell. disput.*, p. 29 and 30; *post.*, part 2, p. 143; *gülden Griff.*, p. 63.) (2) *He strips it of every effectiveness*: [15] "The letter is not the vehicle of the Word," "One does not learn about God from the letter," "The letter is not the seed of the Church. We do not elicit the truth from it," "The ministry of the Word is fruitless, for the Word stays on its paper and in its churches of stone. It causes only worldly faith - *Weltglaube*," "We do not seek faith and judgment about spiritual matters from the letter of Scripture," "It is not the letter, but God, who creates the children of God," and, finally, "If we must know the sense of Scripture, we must abandon Scripture, be ignorant of its literal meaning and enter into the virtue [or power] of the Lord." (See Weigel, part 1, *post.*, p. 163; part 2, p. 26, 37 and 39; part 3, p. 84; *gülden Griff.*, p. 39, 55, 58 and 59; *von der gelassenheit*, p.7 and 17.) (3) *He affirms that the literal meaning is harmful to the Christian*, that sermons on the literal meaning cause more obstacles and damage, and thus he commands Christians to flee [the literal meaning]. All sects, schisms and heresies begin from a denial of the internal Word (that is, from the word of [personal] revelation) through the dead letter according to Weigel (*post.*, part 3, p. 85, and *dialog.*, p. 55). (4) *He commands us to learn from Scripture by investigation of its sense*. "If someone does not understand something and desires to learn how to make a judgment, he should stand in an abandonment of himself, that is, he should leave

---

39 *sensum literalem*

himself and rest upon his own reason. He should seek energetically the art from God and listen to what God is going to say to him." (See Weigel, *von der gelassenheit*, p. 17.) (5) *He, then, who restricts the literal meaning of Scripture* and does not penetrate the bark into the interior and who insists on the letter we call by way of contempt "*Buchstebler, Buchstäbische Lehrer, Diener des Buchstabens*, etc.," according to Weigel (*post.*, part 32, p. 34, 199, 225, 226, 233; and *gülden Griff.*, p. 51 and 56).

## XXXVIII

Second,[40] *the theology of Paracelsus commands one to bring in a meaning to Scripture.* This one does both by denying a meaning to Scripture or the Bible (*libell. disput.*, p. 17) and by recommending a spiritual meaning. This is the endless complaint of Weigel and his associates: that preachers and those who teach theology in the academies keep busy with the bark in interpreting the prophetic utterances but do not penetrate to the Spirit and to the inner parts of the texts. On the contrary, they recommend a ministry not of the letter but of the spirit (*post.*, part 2, p. 66 and 67) because that is effective (p. 26) and befits the New Testament (p. 243 and 352, and *libell. disput.*, p. 23). [16]

## XXXIX

If you should ask what that "spirit" is, what those inner matters are, what a spiritual meaning is, you will not find a simple description. Nevertheless, examples of interpretation will explain this more easily. Let us offer some here, such as Psa. 110:1. Here he explains the words *Sit at My right hand* spiritually, in this way: *Come down and be born, O Man, and redeem humankind in Your assumed human nature, similar in behavior and appearance to the Adamitic man, until I subject all your enemies to your power even to the final death of your enemies* (Weigel, *post.*, part 1, p. 8). Rom. 10:17: *Faith comes from hearing*, namely, *from an inner hearing* (*post.*, part 3, p. 63). In John 19:26, Mary is said to be *the mother of John according to a new and heavenly birth* (*ibid.*, p. 81). 1 Cor. 13:10: *When that which is perfect is come, that which is in part shall be done away. That is, when*

---

40 The first point was in ⟨XXXIII.

*the kingdom of God is come to me, I shall find and feel in myself and shall taste God, who is perfect, good and true. I disdain everything which is in part; that is, I shall deny my very self by despising myself and by comparing all those creatures to the incomprehensible treasure which I see, etc.* (philos. mystic., p. 149.) Psa. 90:12: *Teach me to take note that I must die that I may depart as a wise person; that is: I beseech You to love me, etc. Seek me out and may You listen attentively to my wisdom* (phil. myst., p. 154). Mat. 15:11: *What enters his mouth does not defile a person, that is, that which is outside my heart* (Moreover, he is speaking about Christ not by imputation but by essential and justifying indwelling.) *neither cleanses nor defiles me; it neither saves nor condemns me* (phil. myst., p. 226). Very many more of this kind occur in the writings of Weigel and bear witness of this evangelical homily that the spiritual sense[41] which he is extolling to such an extent is some kind of allegory.

## XL

Indeed, we know that the Scriptures of the New Testament sometimes shapes allegories from the prophetic texts (as in Gal. 4:22 and Rom. 10:6 and 7), and this especially from the comparison of type and antitype (as in Col. 2:17, and Heb. 8:1); therefore, let us not impugn allegories [17] which are applied for the further clarification of matters, especially because the apostles used this method of teaching, although sparingly and not as the ordinary procedure for interpreting which makes for all clarification of things proved but not for the foundation of dogmas.

## XLI

But yet we offer no support to Weigel as he creates this one true, genuine, and ordinary way of interpreting theology because, first, we have no command to seek out this meaning in any Scripture; second, he cannot show how that way flows out from the text even as we are now thinking about this; third, it is the speculation of our reason and the application, often violent, of the texts, and twisted arbitrarily for any purpose whatsoever; fourth, therefore it is multifaceted in proportion

---

41  *sensum spiritualem*

to the good pleasure of this or that person in forming it; fifth, a person's conscience can never claim to itself with certain infallibility that those meanings have proceeded from God; sixth, that method of interpretation convicts itself because its own preconceived notion of theology is the creator thereof. For this reason, it surely is necessary for us to admit that the spiritual meanings are, so to speak, attached[42] to Scripture, and that the person who commands that people follow them as they reject the literal meaning is bringing into Scripture a meaning which he has taken from some other source.

## XLII

Third,[43] *that theology disapproves of the real means of interpretation.* The apostolic rule is: *God's workman will correctly divide the word of truth* [2 Tim. 2:15]. This rule requires both an organized arrangement and a distinction of various subjects so that one does not confuse Law and Gospel, justification with a consequent pursuit of sanctification, threats with promises, etc.

## XLIII

The theology of Paracelsus also does not approve of this instruction of the apostle. Weigel writes as follows (*dial. de Christ.*, p. 38): *When I formerly used to attend schools, I learned such matters, and now every day I am hearing from the pulpit that faith is one thing, Christ another, His life another, repentance another, confession another, justification another, new obedience or satisfaction another, baptism another,* [18] *regeneration or the new creation another, the Spirit another, the keeping of the Lord's commandments another, the divine Law another, the Gospel another, etc. But I am speaking in truth as long as I am not departing from this truth nor from human theology, so long as I am not bringing all things together in Christ and including Jesus Christ with the cross, etc. They are acknowledging and preaching Christ only in half measure, and are denying the work, virtue and life of Christ, etc. Also: The learned, worldly professors in the academies don't want people to confuse these*

---

42 *affingi*
43 The first point was in ❡XXXIII.

*matters* (faith, prayer, confession, repentance and justification) *with each other but distinguished by dialectics, that they may teach people all the better in the business of faith as they pretend that they are correctly dividing the Word. For this reason they are not following Christ but human reason, etc. They are separating one thing from another because faith is one thing, prayer another, confession another, conversion another, repentance another, etc. according to the letter and the external man. This may be the situation, but what does this have to do with us Christians who in all things live according to spirit and truth?* (See his *postilla*, part 2, p. 217.)

## XLIV

We draw this conclusion. Whoever is not willing to rightly divide the Word nor to distinguish those things which differ very greatly is removing the true means and method of the interpretation of theology. This is what Weigel, the defender of Theophrastus, is doing, as we have just proved. Therefore he is also removing the true method of theological interpretation.

## XLV

Now that we have proved the three parts of the minor premise in the syllogism, we conclude that the theology of Paracelsus is not bound to Scripture in the interpretation thereof. From what we have proved, it further follows that the Paracelsists are not bound to Scripture either, first, in establishing dogmas or, second, in interpretation. The same people also are not making Holy Scripture the active principle of theological cognition, and that is what we had to prove. [19]

## XLVI

Second,[44] CHRIST. Christ is the other primary teaching cause as we consider Him especially by reason of His office, as a Prophet once recommended many times *through the prophets*. Deu. 18:15: "The Lord, your God, will raise up unto you from the midst of you, of thy brethren

---

44  The "first" here goes back to ¶ XI.

like unto me, and unto Him you will hearken," Isa. 50:4: "The Lord God has given me the tongue of the learned that I might know how to sustain with a word the person who has fallen." Isa. 61:1–2: "The Spirit of the Lord is upon me for He has anointed me to preach to the meek that I may ease those of a contrite heart, to preach forgiveness to the captives and open the prisons to proclaim the acceptable year of the Lord," etc. He was also recommended *by the voice of the heavenly Father*, Mat. 17:5: "This is My beloved Son, in whom I am well-pleased. Hear ye Him." *He Himself*, however, calls people to be His disciples, as in Mat. 11:29: "Learn from Me." We find an emphasis on the prophetic office of Christ which, just as other matters, we must define with broad terms for four years and in that which has not yet been completed.[45] However, because He was sent as a Prophet to we who are still alive today no less than to people of that time, we cannot entertain any doubt but that those heavenly and prophetic words—"Hear ye Him"—bind us to listen to Christ.

## XLVII

Furthermore, the very *manner*[46] of listening is either immediate or mediate. The disciples of Christ once enjoyed the former method just as did others who came together from here or there to listen to Him. For this reason we read that they were more blessed than others. Mat. 13:17: *Blessed are your ears for they are listening. Indeed, verily I say to you that many prophets and just people want to hear the things which you have been hearing but have not heard them.* For this reason, then, we are inferior to them because Christ does not speak to us by immediate act but informs each person about the kingdom of heaven.

## XLVIII

The *mediate* manner, on the other hand, is founded partly on that general command: *Go ye into all the world and preach the Gospel to every creature*; partly on the instruction connected to that mandate: *Teach them to observe all things that I have commanded unto you* (Mat. 28:20); and finally,

---

45 Hunnius is referring to Christ's prophetic office beginning with His baptism, and which continues to this day.
46 *modus*

partly on that clear statement of Christ [20], Luke 10:16: *He who hears you hears Me, and he who despises you, despises Him who sent Me.* The apostles were performing their office in this way in the name of Christ (2 Cor. 5:20); they were receiving instruction from the Spirit of truth, who was reminding them of the things which Christ had taught first (John 14:26) so that they did not dare to speak of things which Christ was not causing through them (Rom. 15:18). Therefore, our Savior truly exercises His prophetic office and truly speaks to people, and they truly hear Him as He speaks through the apostles.

## XLIX

The course of apostolic preaching did not bring a conclusion to that office, and they themselves placed teachers in charge of the churches, and they commanded these to put others in charge thereof, which we see in the examples of Paul committing the Church at Ephesus to Timothy for his instruction and the churches of Crete to Titus for his instruction. In this latter case, Paul also enjoined Titus to establish elders[47] town by town (Tit. 1:5). We also see this in the example of Peter, and he committed the feeding of the Lord's flock with the salutary Word to elders (1 Pet. 5:2). From this we draw the simple conclusion that this mediate manner of preaching should last until the blessed Jesus cease to gather His Church for Himself on earth, that is, at the end of the age.

## L

The leaders of the Church perform this office either orally of through their writings. No third method is offered. That office includes sermons delivered in the public assemblies of the Church as well as in private and in extraordinary explanations. The apostles and faithful pastors have directed their writings to the salutary instruction of the more simple so that the person who selects such writings should hear Christ teaching. (Such a person nevertheless should examine these according to the teachings of Christ and of the apostles.)

---

47 *presbyteros* here, and *Presbyteris* in the 1 Pet. 5 passage. This is one of the primary terms used in the New Testament for referring to the pastoral office.

## LI

In sum, whoever does not listen to Christ as his teacher is not a Christian; but, whoever does listen to Him enjoys His immediate inspiration, whether he hears ministers professing heavenly doctrine orally or in writing.

## LII

It is not apparent to those who accommodate these points to the theology of Paracelsus that it [the Paracelsian doctrine] *does not acknowledge Christ as teacher*. This we show as follows: first, those people are unable to deny that, when Christ was walking about on earth in a visible way when He was carrying out His ministry, He was teaching. [21] Second, they do not dare affirm that the Lord Jesus taught anything when He appeared to people either in dreams or otherwise. We do not read this in their writings. Therefore they have denied both of these things and profess that Christ does not teach them immediately. They say that He united the remaining mysteries to His essential self. However, as soon as that essential union was disapproved, the secret matter fell freely, and this they call "instruction." Others, however, have taught these points concerning this subject elsewhere.

## LIII

*They do not acknowledge the mediate manner of hearing.* They do not listen to the living voice of the apostles, and they neglect their writings (especially because they remove from them the certainty of what they teach, as Weigel writes, *gülden Griff.*, p. 57: *It is not enough for him to consider that the Holy Spirit could not err. Tell me, do you first prove this as true? You will prove and defend it only with difficulty.* "Who is Cephas? Who is Apollos? Who is Paul?," *the apostle says. Who is this or that person? They are only people. It is God, God, God, who is the only God, who alone works faith and gives the judgment to test every spirit and all writings.*). They disrespect the successors of the apostles either as preachers or as writers and forbid people to listen to them, as they even now teach. Therefore the Paracelcist theology does not enjoy this second prophetic office of Christ, and therefore clearly no manner thereof. Instead, it lacks this chief Teacher of the Church[48] and the founder of genuine theology.

## LIV

We therefore draw this conclusion. *The theology of Paracelsus does not hear Christ when He teaches by reason of His prophetic office. Therefore it does not permit the active principle of theological understanding to exist. As a consequence, it rejects the true and primary cause of teaching.*

---

48 *hoc primario Ecclesiæ doctore*

## CHAPTER III
## On the organic and ordinary cause of theological instruction which the school of Paracelsus does not admit.

I

That God uses means in teaching humankind we have just shown. This, however, is the condition of the instrument that the primary cause works something through that. This does not flow into the subject matter spread beneath the action unless the instrument has been applied to that matter. [22]

II

Therefore, whatever God accomplishes in people as His disciples, through people, these do not become partners of His unless there be some union of both the teachers and of the learners, and this is nothing else but the hearing supplied to those who teach others according to the divine command and their calling.

III

Those teachers are in control of either a private organization in the domestic arrangement where parents teach their children (Eph. 4:1, 1 Tim. 5:14); or in a public organization, and again there are two here—schools and churches. *In the churches*, the minister of the Word teaches the entire assembly from his pulpit. *The schools* are either common[49] or academic, and in these the youth learn more carefully the foundations of godliness and good literature and are made ready for the preaching of the Word. If, however, you are speaking about the legitimate use thereof, all these are the workshops of the Holy Spirit.

---

49 *triviales*

## IV

I say "legitimate use" because just as some serious abuse comes to any laudable institutions, especially to the divine Word, and this we must detest very much; so also is the situation in the schools in which some stubborn and rash students have been listening to Satan teaching under the darkness of the papacy. Academies or churches are schools instilling the poison of Antichristian and other heresy into our youth. As a result, they are the schools of Satan (Rev. 3:9), from which Christ is an utter exile. Therefore, all Christians detest these, and justly so.

## V

In the meantime, however, abuse should not remove use. Rather, let us separate the precious from the cheap and test all the spirits whether they are of God, whether they have received some place in the schools or in the churches. If we detect that schools or churches are professing salutary matters, we must certainly regard them as instruments of the Holy Spirit from which we must seek instruction in faith and works.

## VI

However, *the school of Paracelsus rejects these instrumental causes of theological institution*, not only by *rejecting* them purely and directly and by asserting that *no one is produced as a truly and solidly learned man from a mortal teacher*, as Theophrastus argues (Bk.1, *de podag.*, Vol. 4, p. 254); but also by denying most of them through clear consequences.

## [23] VII

*The school of Paracelsus, first, denies a divine calling.* Everyone who presumes to teach the Church must have the equipment of a divine calling according to that statement of Rom. 10:15: *How will they preach unless they be sent?* The school of Paracelsus, after positing this as being beyond doubt, assumes that the professors of academies, the preachers of the Church, and the moderators of schools have no call from God. Weigel (*post.*, part 1, p. 44): *Faithful preachers should be the angels of God, that is, God should have taught and sent them, and not people. You see, they themselves are running without having been called to preach. They are mercenaries such as we all are now without exception, for whom of us has God instructed, and who allows himself to have God call him? Or, have all of us been established on the basis of academic favor and human power?* Part 2, postil., p. 31: *Those whom people have chosen and called do not bring with them the Holy Spirit. Their preaching and absolution are of no value. They speak and bear witness like a person who is color-blind. They preach human dogmas and not Christ crucified.* Dialog de Christ., p. 71 and 72: *You are a learned person but it has not been the Holy Spirit who has moved you forward, but the academies, where no one has been found to be of the Holy Spirit, where no one has been found to have been called or sent by God, but ordained, chosen and established by human beings. You therefore cannot teach spiritual subjects.* The same author has more of the same in his *post.*, part 1, p. 222, part 2, p. 105, 166, 219 and 217, and in part 3, p. 11 and 60. We have prepared our conclusion. The school of Paracelsus rejects all the ministers of God wherever we find that people have established them.

## VIII

Second, that school denies that persons have been equipped with necessary qualities. The Paracelsists reject the ministers of the churches and professors of the schools by denying that the Spirit has equipped them with the necessary qualities and gifts, and consequently reject the office which they are performing. There are four things which they especially demand. *First, God has taught him.* It is certain and obvious that the person who is going to teach others must first be equipped with the necessary erudition (Sir. 18:19). If someone does not have this, he cannot transfer learning to someone else. Indeed, no unlearned person will instruct others because he must teach the divine commandments and not human dreams. It surely is necessary that any preacher be God-instructed[50] because we obtain divine matters solely from God. For this reason, our Savior is unwilling to send out into the world unlearned disciples, Acts 14 and 2:3. [24]

---

50 Θεοδίδακτον

## IX

So then, Weigel (*post.*, part 1, p. 222) writes: *Who of us preachers, therefore, can say that God has taught him?* Part 3, p. 6: *It is clear that no one admits to being God-instructed, but the academies call them all.* (For more of this ilk, see part 2, p. 278, *dialog. de Christ.*, p. 32, *gülden Griff.*, p. 73.) Hence, all who have professed theology and are striving eagerly for both schools and churches are "*Weltgelehrte* [world-taught]" (Weigel, *disp.*, p. 32).

## X

Second,[51] *Every interpreter of the prophets (and apostles) and each commentator on the books of the prophets and apostles must be so enlightened and instructed by the Spirit of prophecy, as well as the writers whose text he is trying to make clear and explain. That he may make the Savior clear, it is necessary that this happen through those who have the prophetic Spirit, who see and know Christ and who point Him out with their fingers,* is the axiom of Weigel (*libell. disput.*, p. 45). He says the same thing in *postil.*, part, p. 19. The assumption is obvious because to no one of those who teach publicly does that illumination come in as great a way as it came to the prophetic and apostolic writings. No one can boast of having the prophetic Spirit, and there will be no one of all those who are performing the office of teaching in the Christian world to preach Christ and interpret Holy Scripture.

## XI

Third, this is the cause of the non-fruit-bearing sermons everywhere—*that sins corrupt them*—because none of our preachers, or just a very few, can say: "Who charges me about sin?," Weigel judges (*post.*, part 1, p. 221). If this is true, there will not be a single one of the mortal race who teaches theology fruitfully.

---

51 The second of four things demanded by the Paracelcists (see  VIII).

## XII

Fourth, *not to be filled up with learning*. Weigel (*post.*, part 3, p. 4): *The reason why Christ does not use the powerful nor the learned from the synagogue, nor the wealthy, but the poor, the unlettered, the contemptible, the people who work with their hands, fishermen is because He wants to have suitable and fitting preachers and powerful apostles. The rich and learned would have been most unsuitable for this and useless for preaching the Gospel. If he had adopted them* [as His preachers], *He would have been in need for them as if He had commended the preaching of the cross to the devil.*

## XIII

*Third,*[52] it advises us to avoid their workshops, and this in two ways: *church buildings and lecture halls*. It indeed admonishes us to visit *church buildings* but not without another person [25] although you may use them as an example (*postil.*, part 1, p. 124). Otherwise, they censure the same as being like shops when by way of contempt they call them "*Maur Kirchen* [walled churches]," "*Stein Kirchen* [stone churches]," "*Menschen Kirchen* [common people churches],""*Steinhauffen* [piles of stone]." They revile the churches because people bind themselves to them and torment themselves with the visiting of churches and listening to sermons. (See Weigel, part 2, p. 329.) They characterize the church and its buildings in such a way that the person who visits them leaves them. They also assert that the synagogue of the Old Testament and the church of the New Testament are opposed in this, that the former were walled temples. (See Weigel, *postil.*, part 1, p. 5, 11 and 16, and part 2, p. 329.)

## XIV

They curse vehemently the *academies* and their lecture halls as they claim that these are the enemies of Christ. In none of these schools and lecture halls, regardless of how many the [Holy] Roman Empire and in fact the whole world has, does one find Christ or come upon the Holy Spirit. In them all the students don't know what faith is, what the

---

52 The first two points were above in ℭ VII and ℭVIII.

life of Christ is. Rather, the truth is oppressed therein, the Holy Spirit is completely destroyed. They forbid the teachers to teach Christ. For that reason, those who are in charge thereof God has struck blind. They know only as much about Christ and His Gospel as do the Jews. These are the points Weigel makes (*post.*, part 1, 93, 96 and 195; part 3, p. 9, 49 and 98; *dialog. de Christ.*), as well as the ideas of Theophrastus (Bk. 2, *de peste*, treatise 3, Vol. 3, p. 185; Bk. 1, *de invent artium*, Vol. 4, p. 256; Bk. 2, *de morb. podagr.*, Vol. 4, p. 313, ¶4; *de caduc*, Vol. 4, p. 6, Vol. 5, p. 164 and 178). I say these are their ideas as they censure the academies although they have very much respect for the faculty of medicine.

## XV

*Fourth, that theology disapproves of the administration of the office.*[53] Professors are unable to instruct the hearts of people by some internal feeling but whatever of this they do accomplish they must do by means of the senses which bring to the internal mind like channels the things perceived within. God and our Savior, Christ, have revealed that process of theological arrangement. The word about God and His will which is going to be restored to humankind through Christ is either preached orally or is revealed to those who read it in Scripture. This the heart perceives by means of an angelic voice or by seeing or hearing, and thus it is moved thereby as if by divine power and is converted. [26] It is in this way that exercises in *debate*[54] come into the academies which prepare students for serious conflicts with their adversaries.

## XVI

That process displeases the school of the Paracelsists, and, *first*, for that reason they reject *sermons* because they agree that Christ is not preached externally (for Weigel counts this among the requirements of a true teacher that he not preach Christ externally, *post.*, part 1, p. 18). That school does not believe that one obtains the kingdom of heaven and its gifts through the hearing of His statements (*post.*, part 2, p. 85).

---

53 The prior three points are found in ¶VII, ¶VIII, and ¶XIII.
54 *disputatoria*

In fact, it sees nothing on the cursed thrones of the pestilence[55] except Pharisaic persuasions which are judged of greater worth than is God along with all His chosen ones, to whom He has revealed the secrets of His nature. (See Theophrastus, *de pestil.*, treatise 2, Vol. 3, p. 74.) Consequently, they judge that we must not disapprove of these who neglect attending church (*post.*, part 1, p. 124).

## XVII

Second,[56] they reject *the reading of books* whether those are books of the Bible, about which we have already spoken, or the reading of those which the leaders of the churches and schools have written for the instruction of their pupils or for the refutation of the heterodox, for they revile such books strangely and not without the most grievous falsehoods and insults as they call them "Human interpretations, *menschliche Auszlegung*" or "*menschen Bücher* - human books," upon which people must depend—anything in which people must believe according to the will and good pleasure of that theological school. They say, on the other hand, that we must not learn from the letter or from books, and that we should not seek saving faith on paper or else ours will be a paper faith.[57] In sum, "the pseudo-theologian Antichrist will find his faith on paper and in someone's mouth," as Weigel says (*postil.*, part 1, p. 96; part 3, p. 18 and 76; γνωθ. σεαυτ., part 1, p. 6). Theophrastus feels the same (*labyrintha medic.*, Vol. 2, p. 174).

## XVIII

They consider in the same number, third,[58] the *exercises of debate* which are outstanding tools for the investigation of the truth and useful preparations with which to prepare learners for serious disagreements. Among his requirements for a student, Weigel has also this: that the student totally avoid all argument and debate, because one does not grasp the truth by debating, but rather hinders the study of theology and causes each student to become most inept in acquiring the knowl-

---

55  *in maledictis pestilentiæ cathedris*
56  Following the first point in the preceding paragraph.
57  *fides papyracea*
58  Following the two points of the preceding two paragraphs.

edge of theology (*libell. disput.*, p. 1, 3, 5 and 39). [27]

## XIX

*Fifth*,[59] *the school of Paracelsus removes every effective operation from the office*—*even when one administers it skillfully*. These, then, are the emblems [of the Paracelsists]. "External things do not save." "Sermons do not send the Word and faith into a person's heart but only stir up the things concealed in the heart. They have neither strength nor power." "Mere accounts of Christ do not infuse the Holy Spirit into one's mind." "All sermons are empty and useless unless there be an internal preacher, for all things must come from within a person. The Holy Spirit, on the other hand, accomplishes all His work without the external Word and not through external means." "Sermons are exterior sheep's noises which fill the ears." "All writers hope to take within themselves faith by reading or listening, an attempt which is unsuccessful, for no one becomes a solid and steadfast Christian by hearing. *Von hören und sagen wird kein Felsman.*" "Scripture saves no one." "Those whom men teach do not know Christ." "Hearing sermons, attending church, receiving baptism, etc. are impediments to salvation. Certainly the person who allows himself to be enticed into the hearing of sermons, attending church, etc. cannot be converted within himself (for the royal nuptials)." These are the statements of Weigel (*postil.*, part 1, p. 32, 142 and 161; part 2, p. 56, 207, 227, 230, 238, 307, 308 and 316; part 3, p. 13; *dial de Christ.*, p. 27, 28, 31 and 33); and of Theophrastus (*de caduc.*, ¶3, Vol. 3, p. 347).

## XX

All these matters, however, bear witness that they disapprove of the ministry of the Church not just because of some abuse but also *per se*. For this reason, **we reach the clear conclusion that the Paracelsists disapprove of the true efficient and organic causes of theological instruction.**

---

59 Following the fourth point, in ¶XV.

## CHAPTER IV
## The false principles upon which the theology of Paracelsus rests.

### I

Lest the fellowship of Theophrastus appear to have drawn its theology from its own inclination or from the suggestion of some evil spirit, [28] it acknowledges that its foundations come from those things which the Church has learned up to this point. These foundations we must not see as different therefrom but as divine.

### II

We find these foundations to be of two classes: some are *primary* and some *secondary*. We say that the former ones are, first, *the internal word which is innate in a person*; second, *divine revelation*; third, *the conversations of the angels*; fourth, *heavenly philosophy* which they pawn off as divine truth on the basis of, first, *the Cabala*; second, *astrology*; third, *alchemy*; and fourth, *mystic numbers*.

### III

They therefore assign first place to the INTERNAL WORD and the LIGHT OF NATURE[60] which contain all things in themselves. That is the way the "new prophets" also feel.

### IV

According to Weigel (*post.*, part 1, p. 160), there is a sort of word implanted within a person, and this is in our heart or on our lips (part 2, p. 129), in silence and in the forgetting of itself. "A person sees the heavenly blessings of all things in Christ with his internal eye" (*post.*, part 1, p. 53). "In each person there is an inherent light from which flows an understanding of all things, and that is in all of us. He who walks in this light does not fall; he walks in the straight and narrow way as he heads to life. Moreover, the person who is opposed to that light and refuses it but rather follows the teaching of men is walking along the broad way to his own death, for he must believe whatever other people say, just as if I were to allow someone to poke out my eyes and use the eyes of someone else. We should not be able to make a mistake nor do wicked things if we should walk according to that inherent light. Indeed, we should turn away from the broad way of men and advance to eternal life along the narrow way. Let us follow Moses and all the prophets, for the light which is within us teaches the same thing as do the Law and the Prophets. He who follows this innate light remains in the Law of God and in every doctrine of the prophets" (*post.*, part 2, p. 184). Christ sends us back to this light when He says: "Beware of false prophets," part 2, p. 185, "because Scripture is ambiguous. Any person who has false feelings can apply it. We conclude, then, that we must have that internal testimony." [29] P. 186, *gülden Griff.*, c. 1, p. 8: *From the stars comes the spirit of man, and from this Adam drew all his skills, works, languages and every living wisdom, for whatever is in a person comes from heaven. In addition, man has an internal soul from God through God's inbreathing, along with the Holy Spirit. For that reason, eternal wisdom also lies within him. We conclude from this that we do not take all knowledge of divine matters from books, but that this seeps down from the person himself.* We can see recommendations of that light of nature in Theophrastus (preface to his book *de caus., morb. invisib.*, Vol. 1, p. 239, 240, 317 and 339; Vol. 3, Bk. 2, *de peste*, p. 184, Vol. 4, ℂ 3; *de caduc.*, p. 346ff., and quite frequently elsewhere). Also, this light is and is called the *Cabala*, or, more correctly, *Gabala*, which the Gabali call a starry spirit which they pretend is within a person, from which he learns all things and teaches that we can prophesy therefrom. This is discussed in great detail in Theophrastus (5, p.158ff.) and Weigel (Bk.1, γνωθ. σεαυτ., c. 3, p. 11 and 12).

## V

[The Peracelsians teach:] In sum, *there is in each person some congenital light of nature from which flows the knowledge of all things. It is a sort of inner eye of the mind which sees within itself all heavenly blessings; and when we follow it, we remain in the Law of God, the doctrine of the prophets, walk in light and cannot err, turn away from the seduction of the false prophets whom we recognize through this means, grasp the true meaning of Scripture and finally advance to eternal life through the narrow way.* This principle we charge with being false:

## VI

*First, because no one has proved a light of nature of such a kind.* Whatever does not rest upon a solid foundation, first, does not cause a conscience to be at peace; second, does not stand firm against the onslaught of temptation; third, does not withstand the attacks of adversaries. Fourth, we therefore reject it with the same ease with which they constructed it. Such is the light of nature. There are two things here that raise our most serious suspicions: one, [the claim] that *there is* [30] in human nature a universal knowledge of all things and so, too, of all theological matters; the second [claim] is that because of this natural knowledge *there is a universal norm of salutary doctrine,* for we do not know when, where, through whom, and how something which the light of nature has implanted has become known to us. We do not know that such a light is the norm of our eternal salvation, and therefore whether we need proof of this. The Paracelists affirm both, but, if you require the fundamentals of their assertions, you will hear nothing about the prior matter, and the latter receives its strength from the statement: *All knowledge comes from within*—not from some book or object. Therefore [they maintain that] we seek quite inappropriately theological knowledge from the codex of the Bible but correctly in the human mind. (See Weigel, libell. disput., p. 12, and 17, and *gülden Griff,* c. 11, 12, 13, 17 and 18.) How shamefully, however, this begs the question and how dangerously they build faith on the sand (Mat. 7:26) and upon no rooted foundation we leave to each godly person for his upright investigation.

## VII

*Second, we charge it with being false because human nature, such as it is of itself and without any special divine illumination, has no light but pure dark-*

*ness.* The topic here involves spiritual matters by reason of which there is a pure and absolute ignorance in the mind. You see, although we may not lack some general knowledge of the divine essence (Rom. 1:19 and 2:14), the mysteries of the Christian faith lie completely hidden thereto. For this reason, we have those prophetic and apostolic statements, Isa. 55:8 and 9: "My thoughts are not your thoughts, nor are your ways My ways, saith the Lord, because as far as heaven is above the earth, so far are My ways above your ways and My thoughts above your thoughts"; and Eph. 4:17 and 18: "I bear witness of this and say in the Lord that you should not walk in the way the heathen walk, in the vanity of their mind, having their understanding beclouded with darkness, strangers to the way of God through ignorance which exists in them because of the blindness of their heart"; and 1 Cor. 2:6–10: "We speak wisdom not of this age but we speak the wisdom of God in a mystery, the wisdom which is hidden, which God has predestined before time for our glory, a wisdom which none of the rulers of this world knows; for, had they known it, [31] they would not have crucified the Lord of glory, etc." V. 12: "We have not received the spirit of this world but the Spirit which comes from God that we may know the things that God has given to us freely." V. 16: "Who has known the mind of the Lord?" *We draw the following conclusion:* Wherever there are, first, a sense of vanity; second, an intellect beclouded with ignorance; third, alienation from God which ignorance causes; fourth, blindness of the heart; fifth, ignorance of the ways of God; sixth, ignorance of the wisdom of God which is hidden in a mystery; seventh, an absence of the Spirit of God, from whom we know all the blessings of heaven which are given freely to Christians—I say, wherever these situations exist, there is no great light through which to see all the heavenly blessings, to recognize the doctrine of the Law and the Prophets, and to find the way to eternal life. Such, however, is the nature of man, considered as he is according to an 'inherent word' and outside of revelation. Therefore we do not see so great a light in that nature of man.

### VIII

*We make this charge, third, because the mysteries of faith lie hidden from man.* This is obvious partly from the statements we have just offered and is known partly from the declarations of Christ in Mat. 11:27 and Luke 10:22: "No one knows the Son except the Father, and no one knows the Father except the Son and to whom the Son wants to reveal Him"; and of the other saints, as Isa. 9:2: "The people who were walking in darkness have seen a great light. The light has risen upon those who were dwelling in the region of the shadow of death." (This statement the evangelist Matthew relates to the revelation of the Gospel which Christ made, 4:15ff.). Luke 1:79: "The Dayspring from on high has visited us to illumine those who are sitting in darkness and the shadow of death." Mat. 16:16–17: To Peter, as he made this confession about Christ: "You are the Christ, the Son of the living God," the Lord responded: "Blessed are you, Simon Bar-Jonah, for flesh and blood have not revealed this to you, but My Father, who is in heaven." John 17:6ff.: "I have revealed Your name to the people whom You have given Me from the world. Now they know that all things that You have given Me I have received from You, because the words which You have given Me I have given to them and they have received them and know truly that I have come out from You, etc." V. 25 and 26: "O righteous Father, the world has not known You, but I have known You, and they have known that You have sent Me, and I made known to them Your name," etc. John 1:18: "No one has seen God at any time. The only-begotten Son, who is in the bosom of the Father, has revealed Him." Acts 17:23: "I announce to you the One whom you are worshipping in your ignorance." Rom. 16:25 and 26 [32]: "Now to Him who is powerful to confirm you according to my Gospel and the preaching of Jesus Christ according to the revelation of the mystery which was kept secret since the beginning of time, which has now been revealed through the writings of the prophets according to the command of the eternal God, etc." Col. 1:26: "The mystery which was hidden from the ages and from generations has now been revealed to His saints." Tit. 1:2 and 3: "Before time began God promised the hope of eternal life and revealed in His time His Word in preaching which is committed to me according to the precept of our Savior God." *We conclude.* First, whatever flesh and blood do not reveal; second, whatever no person knows; third, as he sits in darkness and the shadow of death; fourth, as a mystery which has been silent from the ages and from generations, and in fact, from the beginning of time; fifth, which people know only as the heavenly Father reveals it and the Son declares it; sixth, which people believe through Scripture, through the ministry of the Word, and which has been committed to the apostles for their preaching: I say, that cannot become known to anyone on the basis of some 'natural word' and 'light,' but it rather behaves itself as the salutary doctrine of God which is necessary for our salvation. No one can know these matters, therefore, through a natural light.

## IX

We make this charge, fourth, because man, considered as he is in his pure natural conditions, resists Christian doctrine. The principle of our opponents cannot be the same. Therefore, as God has implanted into the human nature that it should worship God; therefore He cannot impose upon that that people should not worship God. On the basis of this foundation, we are certain that heavenly and salutary doctrine has not been implanted naturally in man if we shall have proved that this heavenly doctrine is opposed and hostile to that nature. We can agree on this from the statement of the apostle, Rom. 8:5–7: "Those who are of the flesh know the things which are of the flesh, but those who are of the Spirit know the things that are of the Spirit, for the prudence of the flesh is death, but that of the Spirit is life and peace. You see, the wisdom of the flesh is hostile to God for it is not subject to the Law of God, nor can it be so subject." 1 Cor. 2:14: "The natural man does not perceive those things which are of the Spirit of God, for it is foolishness to him, and he cannot understand it." We conclude the following. Whatever is opposed to the nature of people, [33] first, by reason of its counsel and wisdom; second, by reason of contrary effects; third, as imperceptible; fourth, as foolish; fifth, as hostile; I say, such things cannot be a natural principle of man, an innate light, and some natural part of his wisdom. Such, however, is theological instruction and therefore it is not a natural principle of man, etc.

## X

This is not that someone may make the objection: *It is at least partly contradictory according to its corruption and also according to the natu-*

*ral goodness which is still surviving*. We do not extend the good and true principles left in nature to the grasping of the mysteries of the heavenly kingdom, something that the antecedents prove. Up to this point, therefore, nature is indeed not opposed to the doctrine of faith, and yet it does not know that doctrine, and does not draw it from corruption. We therefore must attack it.

## XI

*Fifth, we make that charge because at no time has the Church of either the Old or the New Testament paid attention to this principle. She has sent no one back to it* [this principle] *but has always summoned any pious people away from it*. We commend that first point to our opponents to prove if they are willing. Various evidence confirms the latter. Deu. 4:2 and 12:8 and 32: "You will not do what seems right to you, nor will you add to the word, etc." 2 Cor. 10:5: "We bring every thought into captivity to the obedience of Christ." We confirm it with the example of Abraham, who became the father of all believers because he believed, and not because he was in harmony with nature and because that was easy for him to do, but because he was placing no hope in human thoughts, just as it written: "Against hope he believed in hope to become the father of many nations. He was not weak in the faith nor did he consider his now-dead body, although he was almost a hundred years old, and the dead womb of Sarah" (Rom. 4:18). Some who were blinded to the judgment of their own reason suffered a wretched deceit. *Naaman*, the Syrian, listened to the command of Elisha: "Go and wash seven times in the Jordan, and you will receive your healing" (2 Kin. 5:10); 2 Kin. 5:11–12: "But Naaman was angry and went back and [34] said to his servants: 'Are not Abanah, etc. better than all the waters of Israel? May I not wash in them and become cleansed?'" But his servants warned him, and he turned away from his internal light and its dictates and was cleansed (v. 13 and 14. 2 Kin. 7:1 and 2). On the following day, the *Samaritan ruler* was unable to put his faith in the prophet, who on the next day was foretelling an abundance of grain, for he judged from his natural light and responded prophetically: "If the Lord were to open windows in heaven, will it ever be possible for that which you are saying to come to pass?" When the *apostle Peter* was led by the same natural light, he was unable to believe that they were going to kill the Savior of the world (Mat. 16:22). The entire company of the *apostles* were not grasping how the Jews could scourge the Messiah, spit on Him, slay Him, for, although the Lord signified this to them, nevertheless they understood none of those words, and that word was hidden from them. They just didn't understand what He was saying (Luke 18:32ff.). To the words of Christ: "Unless a man be born again, he cannot see the kingdom of God," *Nicodemus* refused to add his support, for they were, so to speak, commending an impossible situation. He said: "How can a person be born when he is an old man? Can he ever reenter the womb of his mother and be born again?" (John 4:34.) The *people of Capernaum* began to judge that the eating of Christ's flesh and the drinking of His blood were impossible, and therefore they said to each other: "How can this Man give us His flesh to eat?" (John 6:52.) Also: "This word is hard, and who can hear it?" (v. 60.) The *apostle Thomas* strongly denied the resurrection of Christ as opposed to natural light (John 20:25). All these things have been so revealed and presented to us so that we may learn in matters concerning faith and salvation to attribute nothing to our judgment and to the light of nature but to abandon these as absolutely false and acquiesce fully to the words of our Lord even if they appear to be foolish. If you go off to the *histories of the Church*, you will indeed find not a few examples of people whom the judgments of natural light deceived but no examples of the saints seeking the divine truth in nature or of sending anyone back thereto to find that truth. However, we cannot deny that the Church has known that it was built on the true foundations of faith, whatever those foundations may be, that she has faithfully sent back her children to those foundations. *From this we conclude the following.* The Church has always acknowledged the genuine principles of theology as such; she has used them and has sent those who are learning to those principles. However, the Church has never acknowledged the natural light as such a principle. [35] She has never used it nor has she wanted to restrict to it anyone who is learning. Therefore, that light of nature is not a genuine principle of theology. These words should be enough to destroy the principle of theological instruction which Paracelsus has invented.

## XII

They assign **second place**[61] to DIVINE REVELATION, about which Theophrastus and his associates write the following. Weigel (*postil.*, part 1, p. 161): "We must listen to unction and the testimony of the Holy Spirit." P. 231: "Preachers and interpreters of Scripture who remain in voice,[62] that is, who listen to the Word of God within themselves, cannot err." Part 2, *post.*, p. 43: "They have and sense the testimony of Jesus within themselves." *Post.*, part 2, p. 61 and from p. 61 and 62: "We are sure that the Holy Spirit must teach us all by unction; otherwise those subjects which are taught or written from within fall to the ground useless. God must teach us all. Knowledge must overflow from within into the object and not seep in from the outside from a book." "Christ wants to give His Holy Spirit not only to His disciples but to all who believe. We have all been gifted with this Spirit by this anointing, provided we are converted from within and learn from Him. In this way, we people who have become learned come out along with David from all our teachers. He who hears many things from Him learns many things from Him. In the space of one hour, that Spirit promotes an uneducated person into a scholar. He teaches languages, makes Christ known, gives one to understand the causes of His incarnation, His death, His descent into hell, His ascension into heaven, and teaches people all the articles without error, if only we allow Him to enter, grant Him a place and, converted as we are, listen to God within ourselves. Then we arrive at His outstanding light and, no person can seduce us therefrom." *Also:* "From the Spirit of God, I learn more things within myself than all the books and sermons are able to teach all the way to the last day" (*dial. de Christ.*, p. 24). "The whole spirit of the perfected is inserted into the Deity, and in a moment God illumines them" (p. 64). P. 319: "Believing is not operating, not working, but admitting that one has been taken prisoner by the Word, that he is resting at the feet of Jesus Christ and awaits the revelation of Himself within us. In this way, we are sowed in a fertile field, grow daily and advance in all wisdom." *Postil.*, part 3, p. 34: "Christ does not make us priests that we may have in Him all things—

---

61 The first point is in ¶III.
62 *qui manent in voce*

[36] a church building, sacrifice, priests. We ourselves can be all things in Christ, our chief priest. All things are being done in our heart secretly so that no one—no people, no spirits, no devils —knows what we are doing along with God, for that is controlled by this priesthood." (We find more material of this same kind in *dial. de Christ.*, p. 8, 53 and 59; *Postil.*, part 1, p. 7, 49, 66, 67, 152, 224, 228 and 229; part 2, p. 6, 24, 35, 86, 87, 89, 104, 131 and 223.) We acknowledge, however, that this is not a true and genuine principle. We are not rejecting revelation absolutely, for this once happened frequently in the case of the prophets but only in proportion to the state of the Church today. Therefore, whatever someone will say about the immediate inspiration of God, we don't want that entire matter to be understood about times other than those which followed Christ's ascension into heaven and particular about the last times. The following are our reasons for this:

## XIII

*First, because God has never promised such an inspiration or inbreathing*[63]*, nor has this ever been recommended as a principal of theological instruction.* We do not believe that there is any doubt that God has given us every principle of theological knowledge and faith, and that He has promised and recommended them. Therefore, if our adversaries desire to overturn this reason, let them produce their own foundations and prove what they are affirming, for we are clearly ignorant of proof of this matter.

## XIV

They, however, bring out two passages of Scripture. Jer. 31:31ff.: "Behold, the days will come, says the Lord, and I shall make a new covenant with the house of Israel and the house of Judah, not according to the covenant that I made with your fathers on the day when I took them by the hand to bring them out of the land of Egypt. They voided that covenant, although I was their Lord, says the Lord. But this will be the covenant which I shall make with the house of Israel after those days, says the Lord. I shall place My Law in their inward parts and I

---

63 *inspiratio, aut afflatus divinus*

shall write it in their heart, and I shall be their God and they will be My people. A man will no longer teach his neighbor and a man his brother, saying: 'Know the Lord,' for all people will know Me, from their least to their greatest, says the Lord." [37]

## XV

*We respond.* This does not accomplish what they intended because He is speaking about the promulgation of the Gospel and is saying no word about inspiration. This is proved, *first, by the fulfillment of the prophecy.* You see, if we judge any prophecy as correctly as possible on the basis of its own fulfillment, we are permitted to argue in this way: A prophecy promises the same thing as the fulfillment of a prophecy reveals its writing. The former, however, reveals no writing of a divine covenant in the heart, which covenant has occurred through direct revelations but one which happens only through apostolic preaching, according to the interpretation of Heb. 8:6ff. Our adversaries have to admit, then, that the Gospel is that second covenant. Therefore, the same thing—but not at all the secret suggestion of God—is promised in the prophecy. *Second, the antithesis of the covenants of the Old and New Testaments proves this,* and this antithesis works like this: *We could not preserve the old covenant, but the new one was being written in our heart.* These are not opposite terms if the subject of the words is the manner of writing, first, because God can write something in our heart, that is revealed therein, which nevertheless is impossible to keep; second, because He has inscribed in our heart not only the Law but also the Gospel. Rom. 2:14: "The heathen reveal the Law as that has been written in their heart." We read that the very voice of God gave the moral Law to the Israelites without any means (Exo. 20:2ff.). The ceremonial and forensic laws became known to Moses through a unique revelation (and through Moses to Israel, partly when he stayed on the mountain, and partly when the Lord spoke to him). Then those became known to the prophets who themselves received very many sermons on the Law through heavenly inspiration. Up to this point, therefore, there is no antithesis. However, that there may be a place for their opposition, we must render the meaning in the following way. The Law was written on tablets and was unable to penetrate the heart. However, hearts filled with sins were too narrow for grasping the Law, and, thus, the covenant made with it was useless. The Gospel, on the other hand, does penetrate the heart as regards the heart which can grasp it. For this reason, we have the assertion that it has been inscribed on hearts and has been accepted thereby. *Third, the use of the expression "written in hearts" proves this.* "To write in hearts" never signifies inspiration but in general, doctrine, whether that occur by nature (Rom. 2:14: "The heathen reveal the work of the Law as that is written in their heart") or through instruction, about the fruit of which teaching Paul writes and notes these among his other words, 2 Cor. 3:2 and 3: "You are our epistle, [38] written in our heart, which all people know and read. You are revealed to be the epistle of Christ which we administer not with ink but by the Spirit of the living God, not on tablets of stone but on the fleshy tablets of the heart," as well at the attentive reception of instruction, Pro. 3:3: "Be not lacking in mercy and truth; tie them around your neck and inscribe them on the tablets of your heart." Pro. 7:3: "Keep My commandments and you will live. Tie them upon your fingers and write them on the tablets of your heart." If you are happy to follow the use of this expression, you will determine that God has promised such a covenant which lies within the very heart and that it lies completely within it, whether this happens through inspiration or the ministry of the human voice.

## XVI

So long as these points stand firm, we explain easily what the same text has in v. 34: "A man will no longer teach his neighbor." If we take this as a reference to the preaching of the Gospel, surely it does not remove the ministry of the voice. Otherwise, how would Christ, the apostles, Barnabas, Timothy, Titus, and others have taught others? How would they have otherwise set elders in charge of the churches? How would they have promised teachers, pastors, etc., and that they would teach the churches until the end of the age? (Eph. 4:11 and 12.) Therefore this prophecy does not overturn external preaching; rather, it denotes, *first, a more perfect knowledge of God* which will come to pass at the time of the new covenant and which used to occur under the old one.

For not only the other prophets interpret that in this way (Isa. 30:26), but also Jeremiah himself (Jer. 24:7), where he changes the words of this text a little and says: "I shall give them a heart that they may know Me, because I am the Lord, and they will be My people and I shall be their God, for they will return to Me in their own heart." It denotes, *second, the preaching of the Gospel throughout all the world.* The Jews alone had known that ancient covenant of the Law (Psa. 147:19 and 20 and Rom. 9:4). Therefore, the heathen who were going to learn it had to learn it from the Jews. This was not so in the new covenant, for then they had to preach the covenant of grace not only to the Jews, but also to the Gentiles, and these not only in Europe but in Africa, Asia, etc. In this way, the Corinthians did not have to teach the Ephesians and the Romans did not have to teach the Cretans, etc. For both the former and the latter had to know God. The instruction of the apostles has this: [39] "Teach all nations" (Mat. 29:18). This they satisfied when they made the Gospel clear and it bore fruit throughout the world.

## XVII

They take the other passage from Joel 2:28 and 29: "After this it will come to pass that I shall pour out My Spirit upon all flesh, and your sons and daughters will prophesy, your old men will dream dreams and your young people will see vision. And I shall pour out My Spirit in those days upon My servants and handmaidens."

## XVIII

*We respond.* First, the promise that the Holy Spirit is going to be poured out in the days of the New Testament (Isa. 44:3, Zec. 12:10 and this of Joel) was given its completion in the apostles, as Peter interprets it, Acts 2:15 and 16: "These are not drunk as you think, for this is the third hour of the day. This, rather, is what was said through the prophet Joel; 'And it will come to pass in the last days, etc.'" We cannot deny, however, that this outpouring ceased after the days of the apostles, and from this we conclude that the prophecy of Joel ceased being fulfilled. Hence we draw the following conclusion. Whatever prophecy received its fulfillment in the time of the apostles completely ceased its existence after that time, nor does any second cause survive to still be in force as if it is going to be again fulfilled. From this, we by no means take a suitable argument in favor of revelations which we are to await in our time. Such is this prophecy of Joel: "Therefore, etc." Second, we cannot deny that this is a prophecy that the Holy Spirit is to be poured out in those times which followed the birth of Christ, especially because, according to Peter's reference thereto, Paul adds his support to his own days when the distinction between Jews and Gentiles had ceased, and applies the fulfillment of that statement: "Everyone who calls upon the name of the Lord will be saved" (Rom. 10:13). If, then, we read that this outpouring occurred in addition to the Christians of the primitive church, we certainly must take this in two senses: first, as a reference to a visible comparison, and then we must assert that the apostles should have conferred the Holy Spirit in this way at all times. Because this did not happen, we must admit that up to this time the prophecy does not extend beyond the limits of the primitive church, and that people are drawing it to today's times in vain, and, second, as a reference to the ordinary gifts of the Holy Spirit with which He adorns either any Christians at all (1 Cor. 3:16), or in particular, ministers of the Word (1 Cor. 12:7, 2. Tim. 1:6). For this reason, we seek no proof [40] of inspiration from this passage. When the Paracelsists are about to reveal to us some third method, let them see it.

## XIX

*The second[64] reason is that because the direct revelation which God promised has ceased to exist, the saints have never waited for one.* In various ways, God disclosed His will to the ancient fathers and instructed them immediately but in an extraordinary way. Thus, it happened that the saints who had not experienced the Lord speaking with them did not await any revelation as about to come without doubt. The reason for this was nothing else but, first, the ending of those promises upon which they could have depended safely. Moreover, what can a person promise himself with reference to God which God Himself does not promise

---

64 The first point begins with ❡XIII.

about Himself? The second is the rarity of revelations because they would happen to a few and not simply to anyone at all. Rather, what was particular was not universal and was quite rare, so that no one except a fool could wait for them. The third reason is the extraordinary use of those revelations. What one awaits is ordinary, and what is extraordinary no one can await as going to be certain. I don't think anyone will deny that this was a unique use of revelation and not an ordinary means at the application of which the Lord would teach anyone. None, therefore, was able to wait for that. On the other hand, because we no less lack the promises, the revelations are divine, if there are any, and very rare, and for that reason we absolutely cannot consider them as a means of instruction or we must count them among extraordinary things; consequently, all the less is it fitting that we wait for them.

## XX

*The third reason is that God denied revelation to people of later times.* We know very well those words of the Epistle to the Hebrews, 1:1: "God once spoke in many and various ways to the fathers in the prophets. In these last days He has spoken to us in His Son" (1:1); and that statement of John, 1:18: "No one has ever seen God. His only-begotten Son, who is in the bosom of the Father, has revealed Him." From these it is clear, first, that God has decreed various ways which we read He once used for the instruction of the fathers, and which He has removed for the future, and from this time He has sent His Son whom He wanted to be sent to people as their final and ordinary messenger. Second, it is obvious that we should not appeal to the last days as if that original way of speaking with the ancient fathers is something that God is going to restore at the end of the world because in these last days He has spoken in His Son. Moreover, as the newest [41] or last things behave themselves as nothing later, so also the final instruction occurred through Christ so that we are unable to expect another after it. Thus, if someone once had respect for that, now certainly no one admits that he is paying attention to a new revelation.

## XXI

*We conclude the following.* Whatever means of teaching is the newest and last of all[65], also excludes all methods which purport to follow it, so that the proper means of teaching by no means allows others to have a connection with itself, even if promoted by some who were earlier among the people of God. Today we must observe only that means of teaching and no other beside, regardless of the title under which it comes. Such, however, is that by which God spoke to us through His Son and His sub-delegates[66] (Luke 10:16). Therefore, we must pay attention to that only and alone and to none other in addition to it.

## XXII

*The fourth reason is that such a revelation is strangely deceitful.* Let our foundation be the Rock of our salvation and not the sand (Mat. 7:26 and 28), for the sand gives way to every mass and does not stand solid in an assault. That, then, which is not solid in itself is not a solid foundation of faith strengthened against any attack lest we be carried about by every wind of doctrine (Eph. 4:14), and like a reed which the wind stirs (Mat. 11:7). Furthermore, that heavenly revelation is deceitful.[67] Heaven forbid that we say this absolutely and simply, for we would call into doubt in this way the prophetic revelations confirmed most abundantly in their own times through miracles and the miraculous fulfillment of what they foretold—as well as other circumstances. Rather, we are speaking especially about those revelations of today which people boast of here and there as they may have shown them to be divine through similar methods. These will remain uncertain because, first, they are the deceitful cunning of the devil. We don't know whether God or Satan has spoken these or those words to us. Although we may think they are consonant with Scripture, we still know that that myriad of evil spirits knows how to transform itself into the angel of light (2 Cor. 11:14). We know that he is effective in the children of unbelief (Eph. 2:2), and in blinding the mind of the unbelievers so that the illumination of the

---

65 *omnium novissimus*
66 *subdelegatos*
67 *Cæterum: cælestis illa revelatio fallax est*

Gospel of the glory of Christ does not shine upon them (2 Cor. 4:4). We also know that it happens frequently that God leaves to just judgment those with itching ears and how and whom new doctrines take captive, as He passes over the effective error that they are believing a lie and that all [42] are judged who have not believed the truth (2 The. 2:11 and 12). The second reason is the vanity of our reason and dreams. Where there are very many dreams, there are even more vanities (Ecc. 5:6). Like someone who is grasping a shadow and pursuing the wind, so is he who takes careful note of the lies he has seen (Sirach 24:2). Therefore, as many mysteries as are revealed in dreams, these until now have been entangled in doubt, whether they are divine or the vanities of sleep. Third, they deceive many people who indulge themselves in revelations. This they prove in that very many statements which offer themselves in the account of the Old Testament about the false prophets who boast of the revelations of the Lord. A lying spirit deceived the four hundred prophets of Ahab, although they believed that they had received inspiration from God (1 Kin. 22:19 and 21). The Lord threatened through Isaiah (29:10) to close and blind the eyes of those were seeing visions. For this reason, it happened that those who gave them credence were very shamefully deceived, just as the Lord had foretold was going to happen (Jer. 14:13, 27:9ff. and 16ff., 29:8ff. and Lam. 2:14). There have been many under the New Testament who boasted of ecstatic revelations and greatly deceived both themselves and others. Let us supply examples taken from the Mohammedans and the Anabaptists of the monasteries about whom Sleidanus (Bk. 10, *Commentaries*) says that they draw any wise person away from committing himself to so uncertain a foundation or to which he himself persuades others to commit their eternal salvation.

## XXIII

*The fifth reason is that the revelations are not confirmed by those means by which God is in the habit of strengthening what He has revealed.* There are four such means. *First is some inner majesty* which convinces not only those who see them that they are recognizing in their vision the divine truth (Dan. 2:5ff. and Gen. 41:8), but even wondrously persuades hearers of the truth, such as are the discourse regarding the copious supply of food as well as the scarcity thereof (Gen. 41:39ff.); the destruction of the family of Eli (1 Sam. 2:27); Jehu admitted as king (2 Kin. 9:12, 13 and 4); the destruction of Nineveh (Jon. 3:5ff.). So too, Christ used to teach as One having power (Mark 1:22). *Miracles* were the second means, and these themselves, with the singular assistance of God, giving witness to the prophets and which gathered authority for the teaching of the apostles. Ahead of all the rest, Moses was renowned for performing them (Deu. 34:10 and 11). Others, however, were also outstanding, such as Elijah (1 Kin. 18:2 and 2 Kin. 2:14); Elisha (2 Kin. 5:14 and 4:34 and 35); and Isaiah (2 Kin. 20:7 and c. 3). Such miracles were frequently connected with the prophets and, in this way, Moses had the confirmation for his being sent into Egypt (Exo. 4:2). The *third* means [43] was the sending of Gideon to kill the Midianites (Jud. 6:36); the promise of restoring the health of King Hezekiah, lying near death (2 Kin. 20:11); the destruction of the cult of Jeroboam (1 Kin. 13:3ff.). The fourth means was the *fulfillment of prophecies* to which God wanted people to pay special attention when He said, Deu. 18:22: "You will have this sign. When that prophet has foretold something and it has not occurred, the Lord has not spoken this. Instead, the prophet has imagined this presumptuously and, for that reason, you will not be afraid of him."

## XXIV

Consequently, as we are about to pass judgment on the laws of the new prophets and wither their prophecies or dogmas, we want to observe two points. First, we do not so much connect these criteria as we rather separate them, for, as we know that all these modes confirm only a very few revelations, only one of these [criteria] could be enough. Thus, what do we demand of another beside that one of those? Second, we want to observe that the fellowship of prophets is not so much separated as joined together, for if the criteria we have noted proved that one of these men saw divine visions, they will have accomplished something. Therefore we conclude the following. None of those people who are boasting of revelations, we detect, has been equipped with any means which at one time confirmed divine revelations. Therefore, it is not credible that they received instructions from those divine inspirations. No one of those who have come out of the schools of Paracelsus and Weigel has been equipped with a manner of this kind, despite the fact that they boast of heavenly visions. Therefore, etc.

## XXV

They assign third place to the CONVERSATIONS OF THE ANGELS.[68] Theophrastus magnifies these, absolutely persuaded as he is that we learn all our skills through the angels, whether they are good or evil ones, for with their greeting they bestow divine grace upon us, as he discusses in quite great detail in Bk. 5, *de orig. orb. invisible.*, Vol. 1, p. 318ff.; Vol. 4, p. 354 and 355, and elsewhere frequently. The deceitful falsity of this foundation those who argue know sufficiently from the mode, from the abundance of examples; but, that the matter may become more obvious, we profess that we must not observe the conversations of the angels.

## XXVI

*We profess this, first, because in the designation of people who are to be teachers after the ascension of Christ into heaven, angels receive no mention.* We shall not mention the happenings of the Old Testament which speak about the angels having explained the will of God at some times but in extraordinary fashion, but nowhere do we have mention that an angel was the ordinary teacher of the Jewish people. Angels appeared at the beginning of the new covenant (Luke 1:11 and 26 and 2:9; Mark 16:6 and Acts 1:10), but they performed the office then committed to them with a single address. [44] They were private and rare teachers of a very few, and never were they the public and permanent teachers of many. People were designated as such teachers, and we understand that they received the assignment to spread the Gospel throughout the world and this by prophetic vision (Isa. 52:7, Jer. 3:15 and 16:16); and the instruction of the Savior (Mat. 10:7 and 28:19 and Mark 6:15); and the relating of the apostles (1 Cor. 12:28 and Eph. 4:11 and 12). For we do have mention of the apostles, prophets, evangelists, teachers and pastors who have been appointed to the finishing of the saints, for the work of ministry, and the building up of the body of Christ.

---

68 The first two points are related above, beginning with ⓒIII and ⓒXII.

## XXVII

*We conclude*: Whomever Christ, the prophets, and apostles have said are to be consigned and established in the hierarchy of the Church as the teachers of people and the ambassadors of God through whom we must learn the way of salvation, we must listen to them alone as ordinary teachers. The person whom they have omitted in this number no one should consider rashly as one of those. Instead, Christ, the prophets, and apostles have counted some specific people in the hierarchy of the Church and have skipped angels entirely. Therefore, we must listen to those people alone and by no means approach the angels.

## XXVIII

*Second, we profess this because we have a special warning from those* [Christ, the prophets, and apostles] *to be wary of appearances of angels.* Because angels sometimes would appear to people in the primitive church, the people were already attributing too much to the angels so that, when a voice from heaven came to the Lord Jesus, some began to say: "An angel has spoken to him" (John 12:29). The Pharisees who were defending Paul on the point of the resurrection of the dead, said: "We have found nothing evil in that man. The Spirit or an angel has said something in him" (Acts 23:9). Therefore the apostles had to warn their hearers not to attribute too much to angels. Gal. 1:8: "Although we or an angel from heaven preach a gospel to you other than the Gospel we have preached to you, let him be accursed." 2 Cor. 11:13 and 14: "They are false apostles and workers of deceit. They change themselves into the angels of light, and this is no surprise, for Satan himself changes himself into an angel of light." Col. 2:18: "Let no one seduce you into the humble worship of the angels."

## XXIX

From these passages the following conclusions come forth. First, when the angels teach a person, they either teach this same thing—that

God has destined men for the ministry—or they teach something else. If they teach the same thing, we run back to them in vain and indeed outside the Word of God, especially because this is not a failure of the men who are teaching. Why, then, do they peddle the teaching of the angels as much loftier and more perfect [45] than those things which the ministry of men publishes? If they teach something else, they are accursed. Second, in matters of faith we should not listen to anyone the worship of whom is forbidden. Worship or θρησκεια is either religious worship itself or a teaching of worship (James 1:26 and 27), for the worship and reverence which the Pharisees were teaching we call "θρησκεια Φαρισαιων" (Acts 26:5). So then, the worship of angels or "θρησκεια ἀγγελων" is a reverence which the angels have spread. From this we shape this proposition. Whose worship or doctrine of reverence is rejected is not someone to whom we should listen in matters of faith. We assume that God has disapproved of the worship of angels; therefore we should not listen to the angels in matters of faith. Third, we must not accept the dogma of him whose form and appearance Satan has put on to deceive people unless we note that it agrees precisely with the written Word. Satan puts on the appearance of an angel when he is about to deceive people. Therefore we must not accept a dogma of an angel which is outside a specific harmony with Scripture.

## XXX

*We profess this, third, because, although Scripture explains the ordinary duties of angels here and there many times, we never read that God has consecrated them for the ordinary office of teaching.* Consequently, we appeal to Scripture to make it free for our adversaries to produce tables of this sort of calling and show them to us. In the meantime, we draw this conclusion. Whomever God has destined to teach people He has commended as such a teacher—especially if Scripture has taken pains to enumerate his duties. But nowhere has He commended the angels [as teachers], although He frequently mentions their duties. Therefore He has not consecrated them to the office of teaching. These points are enough to destroy the third foundation of the Paracelsists.

## XXXI

In the **fourth place**, they set the HEAVENLY PHILOSOPHY which Theophrastus commends beyond the heights very often, as Weigel also does frequently in his book γνωθι σεαυτον, and for this reason the latter declares that it must be counted among the Sacraments (*post.*, part 2, p. 115). Indeed, if you should look carefully at this expression, what is more lofty than heavenly philosophy—that is, the knowledge of that wisdom which comes only from heaven and from God? One must make a different claim, however, when you have established the use of the expression as differing quite a bit from this. For this doctrine which we call "heavenly philosophy" has been made up of the movement of the stars and the changes of alchemy and numbers and accommodated to theology. It consists especially of three parts. First, "*theologized*" *astrology*[69] which looks for mighty works from the stars; second, *physics*, which evaluates theological matters on the basis of the art of alchemy; and third, *arithmetic* [46] forebodings of coming events on the basis of Biblical numbers, and eliciting other mysteries. That this situation would not lack an example, *theologized astrology* teaches that miners, the greedy, the usurious, etc. do not share in the kingdom of heaven. The reason is this: in the heaven at which you are looking there are no mountains, no metals, no bronze, for all these are earthly things, as Weigel says (γνωθι σεαυτ., part 2, c. 12, p. 40): "Professors, magistrates, physicians and lawyers are not entering the kingdom of heaven because there no one needs a supporter of a cause, there is no litigation, no sickness, no reading or profession of authors." According to Weigel (*ibid.*, c. 14, p. 49): "Therefore we must consider all the arrangements of human life on the basis of the movements of the planets to which all mankind is subject."

## XXXII

[According to the Paracelsists:] *Alchemy* reveals a spiritual regeneration, and the resurrection of the dead takes place through changes of substances. Weigel writes in this way (*dial. de Christ.*, p. 100): I

---

[69] *Astrologia theologizata*

*thank God that I know by the light of nature the greatest and deepest mystery, namely, death and life, which destroy, crush and annihilate anything at all in its first form; and yet that same thing returns much more noble in form, might, and power than it had been earlier. This I shall prove from alchemy alone, because the life that comes forth from death is the most noble and finest of all things. Also: I make much of alchemy, for it is the gift of the Most High and teaches regeneration which one can see as with his eyes.*

## XXXIII

*Arithmetic* elicits prophecies from the substitution of numbers, especially of apocalyptic ones. For example, the number of the beast is 666 (Rev. 13:18), but the beast is going to hold dominion for time and times and half a time. This is three and a half years or forty two months. After we make a progression of these numbers and various addition and subtraction, they come to 1620. We conclude therefrom that in the year 1620 after the birth of Christ the beast was cast out and some "third age" is going to begin which they call the "age of the Holy Spirit."[70] Also, Song of Songs 6:8: *There are threescore queens and fourscore concubines and virgins without number.* From this come those mysteries: sixty queens and eighty concubines. Multiple these numbers and we have 4,800. There is no number given for virgins, so add a zero to produce 48,000. Again multiply by three because of the divine essence or the three ages and we come up with 144,000, which number we have in [47] Rev. 14:1. This number coming out of the sixty queens gives ten thousand thousands, and ten times a hundred thousand, and these are the kings, patriarchs and prophets and their children in the Old Testament, about whom Isaiah (c. 3) says that the Lord is going to stand to judge, and stands to judge the people. "The Lord comes to the judgment with the elders

---

70 Hunnius' reference to the "third age" touches on a whole history of literature derived from a notion first expressed by Joachim of Fiore (1135–1202 A.D.). 'Joachimite' expectations were quite widespread throughout the Middle Ages and Reformation Era. For an introduction to the rather extensive literature regarding Joachim and the "third age," see Marjorie Reeves, *The Influence of Prophecy in the Later Middle Ages—A Study of Joachimism* (Notre Dame: University of Notre Dame Press, 1993). See also, James D. Heiser, *A Time for Every Purpose Under Heaven—An Exploration of Sacred History*, (Malone, Texas: Repristination Press, 2012).

of His people and with their princes, for you have destroyed My vineyard." In Dan. 7, a thousand thousands were ministering to him and ten times a hundred thousand were assisting Him. These obviously are all the saints in the Old Testament. The eighty concubines, however, are the different nations in the New Testament. The number, when turned over, gives 100,000,000, which is one hundred thousand thousands. These words—when explained according to the Cabala—make the number whose root is eighteen in Revelation and the age of the Holy Spirit. We therefore must write a cipher (0) eighteen times in this way
1,000,000,000,000,000,000.

Although this number is reckoned cabalistically, nevertheless it remains the number of the saints, which number no one can count or grasp, as Revelation says: "The saints were revealed in this way through three ages, and in this way God revealed Himself to all His saints, etc."

## XXXIV

We justly wonder at that wisdom from beyond the sea because it scarcely appears that this comes forth from human talent, unless one's brain is attracted by the satanic arts. But we accuse this of being a religion and a faith, and the principle of being false.

## XXXV

*This we do, first, because* [the claim] *that this comes from God is not similar to the truth, and we do not become acquainted with it through any principle.* This latter [point] we leave to our adversaries that they may produce for us their principles through which they have learned that God has hidden His sacred mysteries in the stars, in the works of alchemy, and in Biblical numbers, and that God wanted us to uproot them in the same way that they created those principles. You see, they teach nothing else but the fantasies of human ingenuity—if not Satanic suggestions. We shall consider what 'great things' they have grasped. In the meantime, we entertain no doubt that they can bring out nothing to support this idea up to this point because they have not even mentioned any evidence which they otherwise may have boasted of until now.

## XXXVI

However, we do teach the first in this way. Whatever, first, is in heterogeneous theology,[71] second, has a union with no necessary or specific cohesion in matters of faith, [48] third, was not commended or used in the Old or New Testament—that is not a means of understanding heavenly matters. This is a certain conclusion or, at least, is involved in the most grievous suspicion.

## XXXVII

Such is the summary of the Paracelsists by which they derive their theological matters from alchemy, numbers, and the stars; for, as geometry is not to be counted in arithmetic, and as arithmetic is not to be counted in geometry; so also, in theological matters arithmetic, alchemy, and astrology are all the more atheological. The causes are the same in both instances. Arguments of proof should be of the same class and not of different classes, for theology knows nothing of its own except that its roots lie in Holy Writ, and the rest of the matters are greatly foreign thereto.

## XXXVIII

Second[72], there is no close connection of philosophical disciplines with theology which God does not unite through some proof or through objects, or through purposes or effects. However, we can name no chain by which disciplines, after so much discussion, come together in such a way that one may establish any processes and summaries at all from one to another according to his good pleasure. In fact, we do not unjustly relate to this the apostle's admonition, Col. 2:8: "See to it that no one deceive you through philosophy and empty deceit according to human tradition, according to the elements of the world and not according to Christ." In the meantime, we also leave this to our adversaries that they prove by suitable means their connection of theology and philosophy.

---

71  *Theologia* ἑτερογενες (This point is elucidated in ❡XXXVII.)
72  The first point is in ❡XXXVI.

## XXXIX

Third, never do we read that anyone has interpreted Scripture in these ways. No one who had foretold the future mentions this (for we are not relating the parables of Christ to this, which we know very well have been of service not to invention or testing but to establishing and making clear). In the meantime, the schools of Theophrastus should feel free to prove this to us if an example of this exists anywhere.

## XL

The conclusion remains: *Therefore, this principle of faith either is nothing or is subject to the most serious suspicion.*

## XLI

*We make that charge, second, because anything at all is caused from this principle.*[73] We are not speaking about the notorious abuse of good things by which idle people turn darkness [49] into light and light into darkness, making something bitter sweet and something sweet bitter (Isa. 5:20), change sweet water into absinthe (Rev. 8:11), but about the sort of use of which you cannot justly disapprove. But, if we must gather from a consideration of the planets who in the world is going to be partakers of the coming kingdom of heaven, I shall proceed in this manner. In the starry skies we find dogs, bears, horses, dragons, fish, a ram, a bull, a lion, a crab, etc. Therefore, all these animals are going to enter into the kingdom of heaven. On the other hand, neither in the stars nor in the assembly of the faithful do we find some shining example of faith or hope for ourselves. For that reason, there will be no one who hopes, no one who has been endowed with faith, who will occupy the kingdom of heaven.

## XLII

If they prove from the artificial mutations of alchemy a manner of regeneration and resurrection, surely I shall be able to prove the

---

73 The first point is in ℂXXXV.

same thing more clearly from the change of natural things. Wheat cast onto a field indeed returns but in a different appearance—of a blade of grass, of a stalk, of a spike; and as one kernel is sowed, it does not return in the same way but in other different ways, not one, but different from its seed. Is it the same, then, in the resurrection? Various changes precede the physical mutation, and these alterations the philosophers call "previous,"[74] changes by which matter is arranged so that later there is a substantial change in a moment. Is it not so also in regeneration? If the apocalyptic number of the beast, 666, is reckoned in so many ways and with the period of forty-two months during which the beast is going to obtain his lordship, the final composite is forced to be 1620. Hence, they draw the infallible conclusion that, under the reckoning of that year from the birth of Christ, the beast certainly is going to be cast out and a new age for the Church is going to begin. Why, then, do the numbers rather announce the year 702 by adding them together, or by subtracting the same total 624? Or by multiplying them by each other speak of some coming year 27,972 after many centuries? If they want to increase this number to a still greater extent, by multiplying by three because of the divine essence they will produce the year 83,916 after the birth of Christ. What keeps them from this madness? I don't want to go into greater detail. What we have said is clear—that they cannot elicit anything from this. [50]

## XLIII

*We conclude the following.* Every principle of faith is so firm and immovable that it is unaffected by any invention of human ability because of that, beside a serious fault and hateful abuse. Such is not a "heavenly philosophy" as we have now shown with a few examples. "Heavenly philosophy," therefore, is not a firm and immovable principle of faith.

## XLIV

*We make that charge, third, because all the points they draw therefrom are uncertain and of always-doubtful truth.* For this reason, they can-

---

74 *praevias*

not cause a person's conscience to be at ease. In addition, we see that they are concluding that the beast is going to be cast out in 1620 A.D. That arithmetic computation they deduce from it cannot be infallible to any conscience and therefore cannot make any mortal feel sure because of the reasons we have now supplied. Anyone feels within himself that what we say is true. Those who are suspicious of those trifles should examine their own conscience and consider them faithfully. Should even the stubborn know that what they conclude in such a way is true? They themselves will discover that they are hanging in the wind and cannot stand firmly anywhere.

## XLV

We conclude the following. *Every principle of faith can make its own disciple unshakable. 'Heavenly philosophy' cannot do this. Therefore it is not a principle of faith.*

# CHAPTER V
## On a student's requirements which the school of Paracelsus prescribes for those who are learning.

### I

We shall now make a transit to a passive or learning principle and prove that up to this point the school of Paracelsus is turning sound theological principles upside-down. Although one may understand for the greater part on the basis of the nature of related subjects what sort of student the School of Theophrastus desired; nevertheless, that we may touch especially upon [51] the matters which will appear to deserve further consideration, we shall add a few points in place of a conclusion.

### II

Let this be first among these points: the casting out of all matters drawn from human instruction. Weigel (*postil.*, part 2, p. 165): *Whoever comes forth from the academies must forget (with Paul) all things and learn again. Otherwise, he is going to be as useful in the Church as is the devil.* Part 3, p. 72: *Paul had indeed learned his skills in the synagogue, but when he was about to preach Christ and become an apostle, he had to vomit up all the same material.* Gülden Griff., c. 27, p. 71 and 72: *Among all the learned people of the world, we find scarcely anyone to give a single hour to the Sabbath, the Lord's day, as he considers divine matters in sacred silence. Filled as those learned people are with their own books, studies and writings, and thus with their arts, they are so far from the kingdom of God that God does not find in them as much time for working as occupies the point of a needle.* In his libell. disput., p. 3 and 4, Weigel relates the account of some expert, Cythaeroedus, who was in the habit of rejecting students who had studied under other teachers either permanently or for a time until they had first unlearned the things which they had observed from others. Weigel adds: *In this way, Christ did not accept Nicodemus as His disciple before he renounced all his wisdom and knowledge. Paul did not become an apostle until he had vomited out everything which he had learned at the feet of Gamaliel. You don't put new wine into old wineskins, nor do you put a new patch on an old garment, for this would be even worse.*

## III

Let that be in the lecture halls of the fanatics. However, in the school of Christ, this would be an unreasonable and inappropriate request. Indeed, the orthodox learn to know those things which are directly related to theological truth but especially to the dogmas concerning the fundamentals of faith. We have no doubt about those matters, above all casting away all error which, if left standing, allows no place for sound doctrine to survive. Or they learn those points which are not opposed to theological truth; and with reference to these, it is false that this school prerequires the erasure of absolutely all prior knowledge before anyone becomes suitable to be a student in the school of Christ, and this for the following reasons.

## IV

*First, it is false because there is no antithesis of salutary instruction or theological science with the instruction of another doctrine.* Certainly matters which expel themselves from the same subject are [52] incompatible thereto; therefore they are counted among the opposites and nourish an utter enmity. Any discipline—for example, astronomy, mathematics, natural science, instruction in manners—which people soak up, to the extent that such discipline is not opposed to the fundamental articles of faith nor is opposed to other chief doctrines, I say, that discipline is not opposed to theological knowledge. Therefore the one does not drive the other from the subject matter.

## V

*Second, it is false because we read nowhere of this as required from some disciple.* Moses was fed with the arts and knowledge of the Egyptians (Acts 7:22), when he was appointed to be legate to Egypt. In Exo. 3 and

4, when Moses received the Law from Jehovah and performed other extraordinary works at His command, we do not read that God commanded him to spit out all the knowledge that he had learned before. Although he would have spent much time outside of Egypt, nevertheless he had learned everything which he had drawn in while a youth and had practiced until he reached forty. That is not credible nor can anyone prove it. The outstanding prophet Daniel was skilled in all the wisdom, knowledge, and disciplines of the Chaldeans (Dan. 1:4) because the Lord taught him through dreams and visions (Dan. 1:17 and 2:19). Therefore, Daniel did not have to reject human instruction of this kind so that, when he was learning, divine revelations came to him from God. Although the rest of the prophets and apostles perhaps were not renowned individually for their knowledge, nevertheless they had learned from the people of their time—priests, scribes, and Pharisees. And we do not read that Christ rejected the prophets and apostles until they had forgotten all of that, for otherwise they perhaps would never have been His disciples. In fact, they were still fostering that error regarding the kingdom of Christ after they had held first place in the school of Christ for about four years (Acts 1:6). Also, Paul, of the sect of Pharisees, had received instruction in the truth of the Law at the feet of Gamaliel, through whose instruction he had become acquainted with the article concerning the resurrection of the dead (Acts 22:3 and 23:6ff.). But who commanded him to vomit up all this knowledge? He had also read the Greek poets, and he did not divest himself of the knowledge of those poets, for he cites Aratus (Acts 17:28); and Epimenides (Tit. 1:12). Therefore, it is absolutely false what they say about this apostle, that *he had to forget all those instructions which he had learned in the synagogue before he became either a disciple or apostle of Christ*. In addition, Moses taught the Israelites, the prophets taught the Jews, the apostles taught the Gentiles, etc. Nevertheless, when no one urged this requirement especially at the time of Christ, [53] very many Jews had become infected with the leaven of the Pharisees, for they were teaching that people must not omit that demand which we are discussing. Stephen had a religious battle with the Libertines, Cyreneans and Alexandrians, people who were highly trained in human wisdom, and Stephen did not demand that requirement of them (Acts 6:9ff.). Peter was debating the Jews who had been persuaded to demand the cross for Christ. He rebuked their sins, but made no mention of this requirement (Acts 17:22ff.). Paul was preaching to the Athenians, and was not only arguing with the Jews (v. 17), but also with the Epicureans and Stoics philosophers (v. 18), who took him prisoner on the Areopagus (v. 19). He had preached at length about the true worship, but there is no word about this requirement.

## VI

*We conclude the following.* Whatever is required of a genuine disciple of true theology, the prophets, Christ, and the apostles required of their own hearers (for otherwise they would have taught without fruit). Nowhere did the prophets, Christ, and the apostles demand of their hearers that they vomit up everything they had known earlier before they learned true theology. Therefore, this is not required for a genuine disciple of true theology.

## VII

*Third, it is false because our Savior sent His disciples back to listen to men,* Mat. 23:1–3: *Then Jesus spoke to the crowds and to His disciples and said: "The scribes and Pharisees are sitting upon the throne of Moses. Therefore, keep and do all things whatsoever they have said, but don't do according to their works."* With this instruction, our Lord did not want to recommend the leaven of Pharisees to His hearers, for He had commanded them before to beware of it (Mat. 16:12.) Nevertheless, He had commanded them to listen to those who were sitting upon the throne of Moses; that is, who were reading Moses first and then interpreting him partly correctly. For this still survived as a blessing in the synagogue (Acts 15:21).

## VIII

*We conclude the following.* Whatever a teacher in the synagogue orders his disciple to learn, that student is not required to vomit up all things which he had learned in the synagogue. Therefore, etc. This is enough about the first requirement.

## IX

The second requirement of a learner is that he not argue. The listener should not argue with his teacher about any matter but should trust him absolutely. The same Weigel urges this in great detail (*libell. disput.*, p. 1): *I say in truth, whoever wants to advance* [54] *in this pursuit of the truth, he must be a stranger to all interest in contradicting and arguing.* On p. 3, he addresses a disciple who is seeking the position of a teacher in this way: *If you are acting seriously and decide to follow my trustworthy instruction and leading-by-the-hand, I demand this of you as a necessity that you trust me: have faith in me and pay careful attention to me. Whatever I have said and revealed, you shall approve of without contradiction, without any enthusiasm for arguing or responding anything.* On p. 5, he repeats the same thing with these words: *He who intends to grasp the truth must bid farewell to all his skills, wisdom, prudence, sagacity and dexterity and abstain totally from debating. He shall by no means contradict his leader in either an insignificant or an important matter.*

## X

All godly people, however, disapprove of that rash enthusiasm for contradiction by which students attack even the truth they know that they might become defenders of the truth or be captivated by the glory of empty erudition, however much truth they may lose in the meantime with their arguing. Aristotle wanted this kind of pointless verbiage to be foreign to his Lyceum, and Paul claims with much better right that we should keep it from the Church (1 Cor. 3:3, Phi. 2:3, 1 Tim. 6:4 and Titus 3:9).

## XI

However, because they totally and absolutely forbid not only disputes, but any contradictions and arguments—even those which students begin in order to learn—we claim that such a requirement is most unfair and unworthy of the school of Christ.

## XII

We make this claim, first, because they show no foundation for it. As it is our responsibility not to make up anything in theology, so also it is not our business to give orders to learners according to our own good pleasure. Therefore, whatever is necessary in the school of Christ, human ingenuity has not made up but comes down from a specific principle, and for this reason we are agreed that it proceeds infallibly from Christ. You see, there are two means through which we can become acquainted with any such thing: first, Scripture; and second, direct revelation. In Scripture, we do indeed read many things about hearers, their conditions, their virtues and vices, but we read nothing about this. I do not see that our adversaries affirm that this has become known through revelation, nor shall we hope for anyone of such stubborn shamelessness that he would dare to boast of a revelation of this kind. Therefore, let them provide some other means which proves the solid foundation for this requirement. [55]

## XIII

We make this claim, second, because we never read that anyone demanded this in the Church. Again, we appeal to all who we read either taught or learned in the Church, and we ask that they show us one of these who avoided every investigation in this way. On this basis, we draw the following conclusion. Holy Writ relates every necessary requirement for a learner which a teacher may demand from their hearers. However, those sacred teachers never demanded that their students simply abstain from every argument. Therefore, this was not a necessary requirement for a learner.

## XIV

We make this claim, third, because all the sacred teachers willingly allowed their students to contradict them, provided that such contradiction came from interest and from uncovering the truth better. From the very many examples we have, let some few be sufficient. Mary disagreed with the angel about the conception of the Son of God (Luke 1:2). The converted Jews argued with Peter about the calling of the Gentiles to the kingdom of God (Acts 11:3ff.). John the Baptist argued with the messengers from Jerusalem about the office of the Baptist and the coming of the Messiah (John 1:19ff.). Would anyone go through all the rest?

## XV

In fact, we even have examples from Holy Writ telling us of those who willingly experienced debates with their adversaries: Christ regarding divorce (Mat. 19:3ff.); regarding the resurrection of the dead (Mat. 22:4); regarding the baptism of John (Mark 11:29ff.); regarding the payment of taxes to Caesar (Mat. 22:4),etc.; the apostles Peter and John regarding their office and calling (Acts 4:6ff.); Stephen regarding the destruction of the temple, etc. (Acts 6:7); Paul regarding various subjects (Acts 9:22, 17:17, 18:4 and 19; 19:8 and 9); and Apollos regarding the Messiah (Acts 18:28). *We draw this conclusion*. Whatever the sacred teachers endured quite patiently not only in their students but even in their adversaries and who we read never rebuked anyone, we must never absolutely and rigidly deny to the genuine student of true theology. But contradiction and arguing are like this. Ergo, etc.

## XVI

*We make this claim, fourth, such a contradiction of impressing dogmas on the conscience more firmly*. The stricken and erring conscience explains its failures to its [56] teacher or physician. These otherwise might have been hidden from the teacher forever. However, that conscience can be helped in such a way after it becomes known where the conscience is stuck. It is obvious that this situation does not lack its desired outcome, as in the cases of Mary and Nicodemus, who with their contradicting gained a deeper knowledge of otherwise incredible matters. This is also clear in the rest of the arguments by which the conscience of our adversaries is convinced so that they accept the truth when that has been proved or are in the judgment of the Lord rendered inexcusable and without defense.

## XVII

*We conclude the following.* We should reject no means which impresses salutary dogmas upon consciences more firmly as if they were alien to the school of Christ. Such [a means] is moderate contradiction and argument, as we have proved. Therefore, in no way should we reject these as alien to the school of Christ.

## XVIII

*Fifth, we make this claim because it forbids the testing of spirits.* We know well the command which Christ taught us several times: "Beware of false prophets who come to you" (Mat. 7:15). "Don't believe every spirit but test the spirits whether they be from God" (1 John 4:1). This demand of Weigel is diametrically opposed to this command because I cannot and ought not test him whom I am to trust absolutely to see whether he is of God. Without any beating around the bush, I do contradict this believing in that very spirit which I am proving, and this I do seriously and with at least a concern for testing it. *We conclude the following.* Whatever of itself directly gets in the way of the testing of the spirits, that is not divine nor in harmony with the school of Christ. The demand of Weigel is like that. Therefore, etc.

## XIX

*Sixth, we make this claim because it demands that which is not in the power of humans, and it cannot allow a conscience to be at rest.* That the human heart would believe without contradiction is not in the power of that heart, for it cannot stipulate except to that of the truth of which he is completely convinced. However, that he may become convinced, there is a need for a great doubt which presses the conscience. Indeed, those matters are not removed if we do not know them well, and we do not know them well unless we investigate them and contradict them with our questions. This is not to mention that believing is the work of God and not of people (John 6:29). [57]

## XX

If one should say that it befits a student with a heart not sufficiently instructed in the truth of some matter, to refrain from arguments and contradictions, what else is persuaded except that he must make a decision in matters concerning salvation, even with a fearful conscience? *We draw the following conclusion.* Whatever demands from a beginner in theology that which is not within his power, or which is not the work of God, or makes his conscience waver and be in doubt, that is not Christian. Such, however, is the requirement regarding the trust someone must have in one who teaches sacred matters. Therefore that requirement of Weigel is not Christian.

## XXI

*Seventh, we make this claim because Weigel himself gravely rebukes (although through calumny) the evangelical churches of forcing students to agree with the bare good-pleasure of those who teach (post., part 2, p. 36, 61, 188 and 180; part 3, p. 3; dialog. de Christ., p. 21; and gülden Griff., p. 3 and 4). We draw this conclusion.* Whatever the Paracelsists condemn rigidly in the school of the Evangelicals or Lutherans, this they urge absurdly in their own school. They condemn rigidly in the schools of the Lutherans that a learner believe anything without contradiction in esteem for the teacher. Therefore they cannot urge this in their own schools except absurdly.

## XXII

**The third requirement is the forsaking and forgetting of oneself**, something that the fanatics render with the fanatic word *"de Gelassenheit - resignation,"* through which a person withdraws his heart not only from mundane matters, but also from himself so that he divests himself of all pleasures, puts aside every concern, dismisses all comfort, attends himself with hatred, sinks himself into silence and, in fact, eventually goes down into nothing. In this way and by this procedure, [they say] the hearer becomes suitable to God as He reveals matters. This is the way Weigel speaks both through all his writings in countless passages and in the special book *von der Gelassenheit*.

## XXIII

There lurks here a profound error and the foundation of all fanatic theology[75] into the power of which we now cut whenever [58] we advise that we should not pay attention to revelations in a point of religion. However, we knock this down in detail in this way. Whatever arrangement for learners, first, does not rest upon the divine will or ordinance nor upon another solid foundation and for this reason is uncertain as to whether God has approved or disapproved it; second, which leads away from the ordinary pathway of teaching; third, which opens the doors to the temptations of Satan; and fourth, which therefore brings on a very present danger to the soul; I say, that cannot be Christian nor necessary for the godly student of theology. Such, however, is that abandonment of oneself, or the *Gelassenheit*. Therefore, that cannot be necessary for the godly student of theology.

## XXIV

We are agreed, however, on the basis of these very brief samplings, that *even the passive principle of theology*, that is, *the learner*, is transformed and corrupted in so ugly a fashion by the Paracelcists that he comes out as totally unsuitable for grasping theological instruction. From this there emerges the general conclusion:

### Therefore, the theology of Paracelsus is not divine.
This is what we had to prove.

### To God alone the glory!

---

75 *Theologiæ Fanaticæ*—Thus Hunnius returns to the title of the work as he draws to a conclusion.

www.ingramcontent.com/pod-product-compliance
Lightning Source LLC
LaVergne TN
LVHW021404080426
835508LV00020B/2452